Quant Computing and Future

Understand Quantum Computing and Its Impact on the Future of Business

---

Utpal Chakraborty

www.bpbonline.com

FIRST EDITION 2022

Copyright © BPB Publications, India

ISBN: 978-93-89423-266

LIMITS OF LIABILITY AND DISCLAIMER OF WARRANTY

To View Complete
BPB Publications Catalogue
Scan the QR Code:

www.bpbonline.com

Dedicated to

Birendranath Chakraborty (Father)

Sikha Chakraborty (Mother)

Suchhanda Chakraborty (Wife)

Panchali Chakraborty Gupta (Sister)

Arup Gupta (Brother-in-Law)

Arnab Chakraborty (Son)

Avighna Gupta (Nephew)

*My entire family, who inspires
me in every walk of my life.*

About the Author

Utpal Chakraborty is an eminent Data Scientist, AI Researcher, Quantum Scientist, Strategist and Thought Leader having more than two decades of industry experience, including working as a Principal Architect in L&T Infotech, IBM, Capgemini and other MNCs in his past assignments. He was also the Head of Artificial Intelligence division of YES Bank. At the moment he is the Chief Digital Officer at Allied Digital Services Limited. Utpal is a well-known speaker and writer on Artificial Intelligence, Quantum Computing, IoT, Agile & Lean speaking at conferences , premier colleges & universities around the world. His recent research on machine learning titled "Layered Approximation for Deep Neural Networks" and book "Artificial Intelligence for All" has been appreciated in different conferences, institutions and universities. He has also demonstrated few completely out-of-the-box hybridized Agile & Lean implementations in different industries which has been recognized and appreciated by Agile & Lean communities worldwide. He has helped and mentored startups in their journey, helped institutions like IITs in their different research programs. He is in the advisory body of many Govt., academia and private research institutions. Utpal has also been recognized as one among top AI Influencers & Thought Leaders by reputed forums. He has also been recognized as Global AI Ambassador 2022.

LinkedIn - **https://www.linkedin.com/in/utpal-chakraborty/**

Twitter - **https://twitter.com/utpal_bob**

About the Reviewer

Dr. Amit Banerjee, Ph.D. Technocrat, Scientific Advisor Microelectronic Technologies & Devices, Keynote Speaker, Scientific Author & Editor, Dr. Amit Banerjee joined the Advanced Device Research Division, Research Institute of Electronics, Shizuoka University, National University Corporation, Japan as a Scientific Researcher in 2016 and was also part of the Innovative Photonics Evolution Research Center at Hamamatsu, Japan. He later joined the Microelectronic Technologies & Devices, Department of Electrical and Computer Engineering of the prestigious National University of Singapore, as Scientist in 2017. Currently Amit is member of 30+ international advisory boards, technical program committees in various countries, acted as panel editor, reviewer for reputed journals and scientific book volumes, Adviser and Lead Contributor: Semiconductor Devices and Process Technologies, EDGE196, Entrepreneur Development Global Ecosystem; Adviser, EntrepreneursFace, Global Venture Capital and Entrepreneurs Network, Singapore; Scientific Adviser to ULVAC Technologies Inc. Japan/USA, Scientific Adviser to ISF Analytica & Informatica, Scientific Adviser to Digivalley Innovations; External Adviser, Bioelectronics and Biomedical Technologies, Ocuro Science and Technology (biomed-startup); Scientific Adviser to Ominar Innovations (biomed-startup);Consultant with Asentrex Global, member of Japan Society of Applied Physics; member of Society for Functional Nanomaterials, by UCLan's Institute of Nanotechnology and Bioengineering, UK; life member Indian Physical Society.

Alongside the pursuit of high-tech research, consulting futuristic technologies for business firms, Amit is keenly engaged in consulting educational ventures and universities: Academic Adviser/Visiting Faculty to NSHM Group of Institutions, Brainware University, Swami Vivekananda University; Arohan Educan Ltd. London, UK; Ambassador, Bentham Science Publishers, SG. Amit received Ph.D. degree in Semiconductor Technology from Energy Research Unit,

Indian Association for the Cultivation of Science (D.S.T., Govt. of India) and has extensively worked on design and development of high vacuum plasma CVD reactors, which are used in industrial manufacturing of solar cells, coatings and TFTs. He also developed low cost high vacuum MWPECVD units, and conceived the process for cost effective commercial grade antireflection coatings (ARC) synthesis for solar cells by nanocrytalline diamonds (NCDs). His current work is on Terahertz Technology, including THz sensors and sources, design, fabrication, aiming at biomedical imaging applications. His recent work on antenna-coupled microbolometer arrays, are compatible with the state-of-the-art medium-scale semiconductor device fabrication processes, and technologically competitive with commercial viability as on-chip integrable detector arrays for terahertz imaging. Amit has co-authored several scientific papers, presented in several international conferences as plenary and keynote speakers, received 7 awards including Award by Quality in Research (QiR), Indonesia; Award in Industrial and Clinical Applications by University of Central Lancashire, UK; Young Physicist Award and honorary life-membership from Indian Physical Society; Award by the Metrology Society of India (MSI); Award Indian Institute of Chemical Engineers (IIChE); Award by Dept. of Atomic Energy (D.A.E.).

Acknowledgement

There are a few people I want to thank for the continued and ongoing support they have given me not only during the writing of this book but to become a champion and industry expert in the field of Artificial Intelligence and Quantum Computing. I want to thank my mom & dad, my wife, my sister & my brother-in-law, my son and my nephew. I could have never completed this book without their support. Also, I would like to thank Nrip Jain at BPB Publications for giving me this opportunity to write this book with them.

Preface

Quantum Computing is the landmark in the history of evaluation of the computing technologies that essentially initiates a complete paradigm shift from the classical approach of computing. In a way Quantum Computing is a blessing for the humanity because it has got huge potential to solve many of the unsolved problems which we have been trying to solve for ages. Quantum Computing is already started transforming the different domains of business and our lives and its impact is going to be further prominent in coming few years.

Applications of Quantum computing are not just restricted to in one domain or field, but it's proliferating every industry gradually. It is already transforming different fields like Healthcare & Medicine, Banking & Finance, Genomics & Drug Discovery, Aviation & Travel industry, Crypto & Security, Space Exploration & Astronomical studies, Chemistry & Chemical research, Artificial Intelligence & Machine Learning, and applications in many more fields.

The book also describes various applications of Quantum Computing in different industries and how you will be able to leverage the tremendous power of Quantum Computing in your own business or domain. You will also come to know the current stage of Quantum Computers build by various companies like Google, IBM, Honeywell, D-Wave, Rigetti etc. and their services available for use in the cloud. Also it pointed out some of the fundamental limitations of present Quantum Computers and their future roadmap.

Coloured Images

Please follow the link to download the
Coloured Images of the book:

https://rebrand.ly/aa21ba

We have code bundles from our rich catalogue of books and videos available at **https://github.com/bpbpublications**. Check them out!

Errata

We take immense pride in our work at BPB Publications and follow best practices to ensure the accuracy of our content to provide with an indulging reading experience to our subscribers. Our readers are our mirrors, and we use their inputs to reflect and improve upon human errors, if any, that may have occurred during the publishing processes involved. To let us maintain the quality and help us reach out to any readers who might be having difficulties due to any unforeseen errors, please write to us at :

errata@bpbonline.com

Your support, suggestions and feedbacks are highly appreciated by the BPB Publications' Family.

Did you know that BPB offers eBook versions of every book published, with PDF and ePub files available? You can upgrade to the eBook version at www.bpbonline.com and as a print book customer, you are entitled to a discount on the eBook copy. Get in touch with us at :

business@bpbonline.com for more details.

At **www.bpbonline.com**, you can also read a collection of free technical articles, sign up for a range of free newsletters, and receive exclusive discounts and offers on BPB books and eBooks.

Piracy

If you come across any illegal copies of our works in any form on the internet, we would be grateful if you would provide us with the location address or website name. Please contact us at **business@bpbonline.com** with a link to the material.

If you are interested in becoming an author

If there is a topic that you have expertise in, and you are interested in either writing or contributing to a book, please visit **www.bpbonline.com**. We have worked with thousands of developers and tech professionals, just like you, to help them share their insights with the global tech community. You can make a general application, apply for a specific hot topic that we are recruiting an author for, or submit your own idea.

Reviews

Please leave a review. Once you have read and used this book, why not leave a review on the site that you purchased it from? Potential readers can then see and use your unbiased opinion to make purchase decisions. We at BPB can understand what you think about our products, and our authors can see your feedback on their book. Thank you!

For more information about BPB, please visit **www.bpbonline. com**.

Table of Contents

CHAPTER 1
An Overview of Quantum Computing

Introduction

It was probably a mystery for many of us that *why science and mysticism have such strong rivalry despite both being in the service of human wellbeing*. They are like two distant islands in people's minds with literally no ferry service. There are metaphors in mysticism about the universe, sub-atomic particles, and human life in general which are so profound, logical, and compelling that always wondered me if those could have been useful guides for the scientific studies. A time will arrive soon when we see more and more applications around us based on Quantum Computing which is based on the real nature of the universe and the sub-atomic particles that our ancient spiritual scriptures had hinted a couple of thousand years back.

Quantum computing has the potential to transform every domain, every business, and every aspect of our lives, and Quantum-AI combination is going to be a bonanza for the humanity. Let's understand how. Google's quantum computer "*Sycamore*" has been able to solve a complex mathematical calculation in just 3 minutes that a powerful supercomputer would have taken approximately

10,000 years. We call it *Quantum Supremacy* in the world of *Qubits* when a quantum computer outperforms a classic supercomputer. Now, you can easily imagine that with this enormous computational speed combined with the power of AI how it's going to bring about a radical change in the way we perceive classic computing today:

Figure 1.1: *Quantum Computer Internal View (Source: forbes.com)*

A quantum computer is expected to be at least hundred million times faster than a classic computer. But it will be completely wrong if we think quantum computing will just bring extra speed because it will also bring some other significant dimensions specifically while combined with Machine Learning. Scientists and experts have already forecasted that Qubit in Quantum and Artificial Neurons in AI are going to essentially rule the scientific and technological arena of at least next two decades.

We also need to understand that quantum computing is not just a boon but essentially, the need of the day because the silicon revolution is slowly collapsing as it has almost reached its limit. The rise of quantum along with AI is going to manifest the whole spectrum of new possibilities in the field of science and technology.

The enormous power a quantum computer possesses due to the fact that it can harness some of the fundamental principles like *superposition* and *entanglement* of subatomic particles that a classic computer is not capable of. We will not go much into the details of Quantum Dynamics in this book, rather let's discuss how Quantum-AI combo can help the businesses and different industries.

First of all, quantum computers can solve the wide range of complex optimization problems in all domains that conventional computing struggles to perform in real time. These optimization challenges are intrinsic in the field of aviation, finance, manufacturing, logistics, drug research, medicine, etc.

In finance, some complex derivatives which are path-dependent; evaluating innumerous paths used to be computationally very expensive and difficult to understand their interdependence; hence, can never calculate the near-real-time with classic computers but quantum computers can easily compute those in real time. This will revolutionize the financial market study and prediction of stocks and crypto currencies.

Quantum computing has the potential to improve radiation therapy techniques in cancer treatment. It can help speed up medication development by reducing the time it takes and reducing negative effects. It will also result in significant changes in the fields of genetic research, preventative healthcare, personalized and precision medicine, critical care decisions, and *"In Silico Simulations"* for diverse drug designs. Furthermore, the much-discussed *"digital health"* can only become a reality in the genuine sense if the power of quantum computers can be harnessed and democratized.

In aviation, Airbus is doing RandD combining quantum and AI for optimization of structural wing box design which is a complex area of flight physics. Other applications pertaining flight safety, optimization of travel routes, travel time are just a few examples. Quantum has already proved to be super-efficient when it comes to optimizing complex flight systems. Also, the dream of building any superior decision support system can only come true when the astronomical volume of data can be processed and correlated leveraging Quantum and AI.

Google and Tesla are already using its quantum computer for its autonomous vehicle project for faster processing of information and hence immediate reaction to any situations. Quantum computing is transforming the security arena or the encryption world. Qubit states will eventually empower encryptions unhackable. The flipside is if a bad actor having access to a quantum computer, then it can literally break any advanced encryption that exists today.

Anomaly detection is a classic application of AI and machine learning in different domains and quantum computing is going to be revolutionized in this area. As per many experts, the day is not far when a meaningful machine learning application will be incomplete without quantum computing.

NASA is using its quantum computer for space exploration, astronomical and weather studies by analyzing data generated by telescopes. Google, IBM, Microsoft, and few other companies have already started using their quantum computers for various studies in a variety of fields.

Quantum can play a crucial role in any election campaigns and prediction of results as it has got an enormous processing power and speed to crunch data and bring inferences out in real time. Similarly, it can solve many Big Data problems by optimizing and accelerating search results and understanding the hidden patterns in a much better way.

Various studies in simulated environments are getting transformed using quantum computing capabilities, like in the field of chemistry, medicine, and genetics to understand the behavior and interactions of molecules and chemical compounds in a better way. Simulations of durable battery designs are already done using quantum computers:

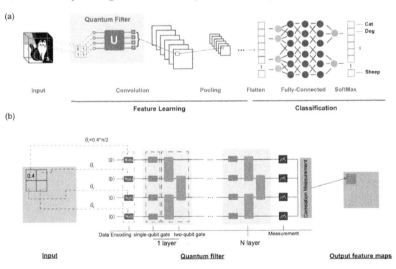

Figure 1.2: *Quantum Computing and Artificial Intelligence*
(*Source: swissquantumhub.com*)

Above all, quantum is going to have the biggest impact on AI and machine learning. Some of the classic ML problems like Linear System Solving can be way faster using the HLL algorithm; similarly, elementary ML techniques **Principal Component Analysis (PCA)** can be done much faster in quantum computers using the LMR algorithm and many more.

So, Quantum and AI are going to be a great combination and will prove to be panacea for many of the scientific and technological limitations the world today is restricted with and has started solving many unsolved facts.

CHAPTER 2
History of Quantum Physics and Dynamics

Quantum Physics or Dynamics initially looks bit confusing to everyone and that's quite normal as per many physicists. The reason being it completely contradicts the established facts of classical physics when it comes to subatomic particles. Many physicists describe quantum effects as weird and strange. The American physicist *Richard Feynman* said about the Quantum theory that was used to describe the tiny objects in the universe - *I am not entirely convinced by the theories of quantum mechanics, but I find them interesting enough to cast doubt on common sense's ideas about physical reality*. This weird nature of quantum mechanics has opened the path for the whole range of quantum applications today, including Quantum Computing, Teleportation and Quantum Cryptography, Quantum Life-Science, and many more that we will discuss in the subsequent chapters.

In the mid-1920s, physicists *Max Born, Werner Heisenberg,* and *Pascual Jordan* developed a coherent formulation of quantum mechanics known as **Matrix Mechanics** or . Matrix mechanics was the first conceptually autonomous and logically consistent formulation of quantum mechanics when was then used for calculations even in Quantum Computers. It was the foundation that was able to displace the Bohr's model of electron orbits. In the Bohr model of the atom, electrons travel in defined circular orbits around the nucleus. The orbits are labeled by an integer, the quantum number n. Electrons can jump from one orbit to another by emitting or absorbing energy.

Quantum mechanics is something entirely different. It's not an improvement on classical physics; rather it's a paradigm shift from the classical field of physics to a completely new field of how subatomic particles behave in our universe. Let's start from the beginning to understand it better.

We all know *Rutherford* showed that the atom has most of its mass concentrated at the center in the nucleus and electrons are very light charged particles that orbit around the nucleus. Also, in the year 1800's, *Michael Faraday* invented something called the theory of electromagnetism. And according to this theory, if a charged particle like an electron moves, it produces an electromagnetic field coming out of the electron. So according to this theory, if an electron is moved a bit up and down, there's a wave that propagates out from the electron, and we call this electromagnetic wave or radiation. This implies that in an atom, the electron should be losing energy while revolving around the orbit. And it should actually spiral toward the center of the atom and collapse in the nucleus very quickly. But in reality, it does not happen in that manner. So, there is something deeply wrong about this theory and the classical mechanics. Now to come up with a proper explanation to this the physicist took a long time to formulate something concrete that how a charged particle like an electron can be stable in its orbit.

The explanation they come up with is that electrons are not particles. They are essentially waves. And the electron is something like a cloud, a wave-like cloud, concentrated near the atomic nucleus. So, this explains the reason why the electron does not spiral in and collapse to the center of the nucleus. *Erwin Schrodinger* also invented an equation to explain the wave nature of the electron called Schrodinger's equation.

Another interesting fact also came out from a serious of experiments and mathematical derivations that the electron is a kind of a wave when you are not looking at it, but it's a particle when you look at it. This is called the famous Copenhagen Interpretation of quantum mechanics:

Figure 2.1*: Quantum Physicists Diagram (Source: Jeffrey Strickland)*

This is fascinating because we and everything around us is made from quantum physics and so the whole universe. These protons, neutrons, and electrons in quantum mechanics are essentially waves. These are also called wave functions to be more precise. Something called a probability distribution which tells us where more likely to find the electron in the wave function. And when we actually measure where the electron is, an electron particle pops up somewhere within this area. So, in quantum physics, we don't know anything with definite details. We can only predict probabilities that things will happen, and this is a fundamental feature of the universe which is quite different from the deterministic universe in classical physics. No one has ever seen a quantum wave because whenever we measure an electron, it becomes a particle. It's called **Wave Particle Duality**. It's called a **Measurement Collapses** the wave function.

This behavior of an electron was first observed in the famous *Double Slit Experiment* of *Thomas Young*. In 1965, *Richard Feynman* described a thought-experiment in which individual electrons were fired on a double slit. Contrary to the belief that electrons will pass through slits and create two similar bands in the wall placed on the opposite side, it created an interference pattern that normally seen in the waves:

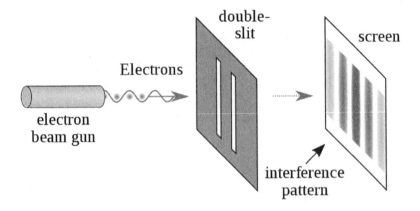

Figure 2.2: (*Source:* Thomas Young's Double Slit Experiment)

The outcome of this experiment essentially tells us two things. Number one electrons behave like waves when fired through the two slits. It also tells us how the wave function collapses to a particle when it hits the wall. And this is not only true for electrons but everything in the universe. So, this double slit experiment has a huge implication on how we perceive the universe in a classical manner and what it actually is.

Also, when we study the interference pattern it forms in the wall, it also shows where the probability of finding an electron is highest which is called **Probability Distribution**. And it is very much possible that the probability of finding an electron at two places at the same time. This is known as **Superposition** which comes from the fact that this wave can be made by adding or superimposing two waves. This feature of a subatomic particle has been used in devising the **Qubits** in a quantum processor in a quantum computer.

Now, let's discuss another strange behavior of subatomic particles called **Entanglement**. When two electron waves meet and interfere with each other and become mixed up, then the interference relationship established between these two electrons remains intake even if they are separated far apart, thousands or millions of miles. This means that mathematically, we now have one wave function that describes everything about both electrons, and they're inextricably linked. Even if they move far away from each other a measurement on one of the electrons can talk about the other. It's just like correlated with a measurement on the other even if they move billions of miles away. This behavior of the electron has also been leveraged in the quantum processor in a quantum computer.

Another behavior of the subatomic particles like electrons is "Quantum Tunneling". Quantum Tunneling is a phenomenon where particles have a probability of moving through barriers, essentially allowing things like electrons to pass through walls. What is means is that when a wave function meets a barrier, it decays exponentially inside the barrier, but if the barrier is narrow enough, the wave function can still exist on the other side, or it can penetrate the barrier. This means that there's a probability of the particle being found on the other side of the barrier when a measurement is performed.

CHAPTER 3
Quantum Concepts and Principles: Superposition, Entanglement, and Interference

Superposition, entanglement, and interference

Quantum computers are in great need when a problem statement involves numbers or data crunching with huge number of inputs that need to be processed in parallel. Quantum computers are designed to deal with complex problems that would take even a supercomputer a very long time to process and solve. Quantum computers essentially simulate the intrinsic behavior of subatomic particles which induces an enormous computational ability that can never be imagined with a conventional approach:

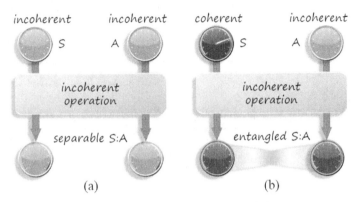

Figure 3.1: How subatomic particles behave

Binary computers based on processors using transistors to perform calculations on the basis of on-off or one-zero. The game changes completely, however, with quantum computers. In this realm, the processing and storage of 1's and 0's of classical systems give way to qubits or quantum bits as the fundamental building blocks of quantum information, experienced as a two-state quantum-mechanical system. The power of these qubits is their inherent ability to scale exponentially so that a two-qubit machine allows four calculations simultaneously, a three-qubit machine allows eight calculations, and a four-qubit machine performs 16 simultaneous calculations.

The three fundamental principles of quantum computing are Superposition, Entanglement, and Interference. Of course, there are other principles as well:

- **Superposition**: It is the ability of a quantum system to be in multiple states simultaneously, that is, the electron exists in quantum superposition. Electrons possess a quantum feature called spin, a type of intrinsic angular momentum. Each electron, until it is measured, will have a finite chance or probability of being in either of the states.

- **Entanglement**: It is a quantum property that takes objects and connects them by permanently entangling them together. It is a quantum phenomenon that occurs when a pair of particles is generated, and they share spatial proximity in a way such that the quantum state of each particle of the pair cannot be described independently of the state of the others, even if the particles are separated by a large distance. The topic of quantum entanglement is at the heart of the difference between classical and quantum physics.**Interference**: It is essentially the concept which states that elementary particles can not only be in more than one place at any given time, but that an individual particle, such as a photon can cross its own trajectory and interfere with the direction of its path.

Quantum computers are built by exploiting the quantum properties of the subatomic particles. But the limitation of a Quantum computer at its core is the Coherence or Decoherence.

- **Coherence/Decoherence**: Quantum computers are extremely sensitive to noise and environmental interferences. Unfortunately, the information only remains quantum for a short while. The number of operations that can be performed before the information is lost is very limited. Knowing in advance how long the quantum information will last before it is out of coherence is critical. To avoid such effects, Quantum Chips must be kept colder than outer space to create superpositions and entanglement of qubits and retention as long as possible. Communication with qubits that are inside a dilution refrigerator is accomplished by using calibrated microwave pulses so that the qubit is put into a superposition or the qubit's state is flipped from 0 to 1 by applying a microwave pulse between two qubits. Microwave signals are also responsible for entanglement. In order to find a solution, parts of a problem are encoded into a complex quantum state and that state is manipulated, driving it closer to a solution but it will take multiple operations to get to the best solution.

When quantum computers provide an answer, it is in the form of a probability. When the question is repeated, the answer changes. The more times the question is repeated, the closer the response comes to theoretical percentage or correct answer. This requires that the code be designed so that the qubits are in the correct state for a given problem. The Quantum code uses wave-like properties that cancel out wrong answers and amplify the correct ones.

As the technology develops, quantum computing could lead to significant advances in numerous fields, from chemistry and materials science to nuclear physics and machine learning.

Like the first digital computers, quantum computers offer the possibility of technology exponentially more powerful than current systems. They stand to change companies, entire industries, and the world by solving problems that seem impossible today.

A recent report by Gartner states that by 2023, 20% of organizations will be budgeting for quantum computing projects. As this new technology develops, organizations will face a shortage of quantum computing experts. There are a very few experts currently in this field although the number is growing as more and more students in the academic world are now taking interest in this field.

Quantum computers vs digital computers

Quantum computers differ from traditional digital computers, which are based on transistors. Common digital computing encodes data into binary digits (bits), each of which is always in one of two definite states (0 or 1). In contrast, quantum computation uses quantum bits or Qubits, which can be in superposition of states. A Quantum Turing machine, a theoretical model of such a computer, is also known as the **universal quantum computer**. The foundation of quantum computing was laid by the work of *Paul Benioff* and *Yuri Manin* in 1980, *Richard Feynman* in 1982, and *David Deutsch* in 1985. In 1968, a quantum computer that used spins as qubits was formulated for use as a quantum space-time.

A classical digital computer has memory made up of bits, where each bit is represented by either 0 or 1. In a quantum computer, a sequence of qubits is maintained. A single qubit can represent 0, 1, or any quantum superposition of those two qubit states. Two qubits can be in any quantum superposition of four (2, 2) states. Similarly, with three qubits, it can be any superposition of eight (2, 3) states. Therefore, one can generalize that "n" qubits can simultaneously be in a superposition of up to "2 *to the power* n" different states. This is in contrast to a classical digital computer that can only be in one of these states at an instant.

How capable is a quantum computer?

Theoretically, large-scale quantum computers can solve certain problems much quicker than any available classical computers. Even the best currently known algorithms, such as integer factorization using "Shor's Algorithm" (Shor's algorithm is a quantum computer algorithm for finding the prime factors of an integer. Shor's algorithms may be used to break the RSA cryptosystem) or the simulation of quantum many-body systems would be no match for quantum computers. Quantum many-body systems can give rise to remarkable collective states of matter that have no counterpart in their classical analogs. Archetypal examples include superfluids, superconductors, and insulating quantum liquids in the context of condensed matter physics.

The current state of quantum computing

If we pay attention to the publications in the electronic and photonic industry, 2022-23 seems to be the year of quantum computing technology.

There are two popular models in which the present Quantum Computers are built: The Gate Quantum Computation Model and Quantum Annealing Model.

D-Wave's Quantum Computing model is the Quantum Annealing Model.

Quantum computers take hundreds of seconds to perform calculations that would take thousands of years on conventional computers. To achieve quantum superiority, Google's quantum computer completed a 200-second calculation that claimed that even the most powerful supercomputers would have taken 10,000 years.

So, it is very clear that Google has indeed achieved quantum superiority and has made progress to emerge as the leading provider of quantum computing services. In 2019, Google announced that it had reached *quantum superiority*, the point at which a quantum computer could perform tasks that would be impossible on a conventional computer, or take thousands of years, or even tens of thousands, which would have been impractical on conventional computers. The company aims to produce quantum computation at a level by 2022 and expects the technology to enter the commercial phase by 2025.

We have seen enough advances in quantum computing technology from tech giants like Google, IBM, NASA and others but the question is when will quantum computers become mainstream. The commercial use of quantum computers has already been started. Google, IBM, Microsoft, D-Wave have implemented a good number of business applications on quantum computing already in the field drug discovery, automobile, finance, logistics, aviation, etc. We will see some of the most promising applications for quantum computing in the next few years.

Given the ability to accurately model and simulate quantum conditions, we are likely to see exponential gains in all kinds of *chemistry* and *nanotechnology* based on a better understanding of quantum mechanics. This will facilitate the development of industry specific quantum solutions tailored to the needs of future scalable quantum computing technology and its application in a wide range of industries.

In 2019, a paper was published on efforts to achieve a quantum volume of 64 qubits for the Honeywell quantum computer. This comes after Google announced that it had achieved quantum supremacy. Google claimed to have demonstrated *quantum supremacy* with its 54-qubit quantum computer in 2019. The Honeywell quantum computer is in 64 qubit. IBM has taken a major leap forward with the release of a 127-qubit processor very recently in 2022.

CHAPTER 4

Quantum Computing in Healthcare and Medicine

The field of healthcare and medicine and specially the Digital Healthcare will get a great boost with the advancement and wide scale use of quantum computing.

Before even quantum computers were there, scientists at the University of Virginia School of Medicine anticipated the potential of quantum computers to understand genetics and diseases in a better way. Now, a team at the University's Centre for Quantum Computing and Computer Biology is harnessing the power of quantum computing technology to gain better insights into genetic diseases through machine learning. Researchers expect that these efforts will benefit not only health care and medicine, but also science and technology at large.

Because advances in genomics are being used to create tailored treatment plans for specific patients, quantum computing technology could lead to truly personalized medicine. One of the most exciting aspects of how this technology will have a decisive impact on the health sector is that it will take medical decisions to a whole new horizon.

In medicine, quantum computing can optimize radiation therapy procedures in cancer treatment. It will also streamline drug discovery by shortening the timespan and minimizing side effects. It will similarly bring about a huge change in the field of genetic research, preventive healthcare, personalized medicines, critical care decisions and *In Silico Simulations* for various drug designs. Also, *Digital Health* which is much talked about today can only be a reality in true sense if the power of quantum computers can be leveraged:

Figure 4.1: For Drug Research

Quantum Annealing ML (QAML), which implements a combination of ML (Machine Learning) and quantum computing as a programmable quantum annealer helps to reduce human intervention and increase the accuracy of data evaluation on particle collisions. Annealing is a heat treatment process which alters the microstructure of a material to change its mechanical or electrical properties. Typically, in steel, annealing is used to reduce hardness, increase ductility, and help eliminate internal stresses. Quantum Annealing is also used for the study of interaction of molecules in bioscience and human body in a simulated environment.

Quantum **Magnetic Resonance Imaging (MRI)** machines are expected to generate extremely precise images that allow the visualization of individual molecules. The Quantum computing technology can improve the MRI technology by providing extremely accurate measurements and allowing doctors to look much deeper into small particles that conventional computing technology would not be able to detect. With the use of quantum computing along with artificial intelligence, it is possible to interpret diagnostic images in its very minute details.

The kind of enormous computing power and intelligence that quantum computing brings will change the landscape for artificial intelligence powered healthcare applications. Healthcare and medicine industry is already in a race to truly reap the benefits of quantum computing; they are in the race of developing several new smart applications powered by AI and Quantum.

Big data research and machine learning are among the areas that enabled in-depth understanding of health outcomes in the health systems. Challenges building a comprehensive healthcare ecosystem require working with a variety of data sources, such as medical records, clinical data, and medical imaging data, doctors' prescriptions, etc. Quantum computers are capable of processing this huge amount of multipurpose data from various data sources, building correlations and inferences to bring a comprehensive view of a particular medical case.

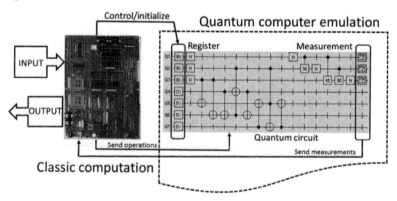

Figure 4.2: Quantum-Classic combination for Drug Research

Quantum computing along with AI is revolutionizing almost all different vertices of healthcare and medicine; clinical imaging, diagnosis and personalized treatment, drug research are just few examples. The impact of quantum computing could be very significant and could potentially solve many of the unsolved in this field.

We have a range of machine learning algorithms that can harness the power of the quantum computing systems to deliver real-time results in diagnosis of ailments. Quantum computer algorithms can generate volume renderings of medical imaging in a fraction of time. This could lead to more personalized medicines based on an individual's genetic composition. Quantum computers can quickly sequence and solve other big data problems in healthcare, and quantum computers can sequence and solve DNA in a fraction of time than of traditional genetic sequencing. These enormous possibilities will lead to the democratization of the quantum computer, as has been achieved with massively scalable classical computing through the cloud. As quantum computers will become more readily available and it will be possible to compare molecules that are much larger, thus opening the door to much faster and more efficient sequencing and analysis of large amounts of data. Quantum computers will release the resources needed to process and understand this data, which means that a large amount of data in healthcare will be sequenced and analyzed much faster and more efficiently.

The same computing capacity that enables quantum computing to harness big data for advances in healthcare can also be used to find encryption algorithms and steal encrypted **Protected Health Information (PHIs)**. Today, API enables programmers and developers to build interfaces that connect classic computers and existing systems with existing cloud-based quantum computers without requiring a deep understanding or background in quantum physics.

The opportunities for quantum computing in the healthcare industry are enormous, but it also presents few challenges. Health researchers are currently focusing on how quantum computer-based techniques can be used to detect cancer. Quantum computing will examine data provided during cancer screening to identify the diseases and also specific cues and biomarkers. There are a number of startup companies that are looking at the computational boost and predicted accuracy that quantum computing could provide in their groundbreaking products and solutions in the field of healthcare and medicine.

Future quantum computers will advance big data analysis by delving deeper into data patterns that are considered too complex. To cope with this complexity, future machine learning programs will require the computing power of the quantum computer system to deal with complexity and deliver results in real time. Together these will enhance the possibilities and advancements in the field of digital healthcare and medicine.

Specially, COVID-19 pandemic has reinforced the need of a digital health ecosystem and has proven that in this highly connected world, we should be concerned about everything that is happening even in the remotest corner of the world because the same can come and knock at your door the very next day. So, although globalization has numerous benefits but at the same time, we should be cognizant about the challenges and threats that it can pose at any time in various forms.

So, undoubtedly the healthcare and medicine industry worldwide need a huge transformation because probably the amount of innovation and agility this field is demanding today has somehow been missing; that's what apparently it has been evident in this COVID time in many parts of the world. The only viable solution to this and many other issues is to build a "**Digital Health Ecosystem**" and Quantum Computing and AI are going to revolutionize the field of digital health.

There are various other reasons as well why digital health is a booming a hot topic. If we consider the cost of healthcare for both critical and non-critical illnesses in a developing country and compare it with average income of citizens; there is a huge disparity, and to bridge this gap the only viable and cost-effective solution is bringing the digital health ecosystem which is going to make healthcare affordable even to the lowermost income groups of citizens. Similarly, even in the developed countries, the money spent on healthcare is enormous and a big burden even for the flourishing economy, digital health is a sustainable solution for this. It can reduce the cost to almost one third in long run as per many experts.

Number two, there is a huge shortage of doctors and healthcare professionals all over the world; the shortage is so enormous that the world will never be able to cater to this need even by producing more and more doctors and healthcare professionals even at the fastest speed. But the alternative is to create a digital health ecosystem with smarter solutions empowering doctors and healthcare professionals with tools and technologies to serve and cater to the larger mass of the population.

Number three, at one hand, there are many areas of healthcare and medicine that have already undergone some level of digital transformation, including maintaining and utilizing digital health records at individual and public levels in different countries. But on the other hand, it has been observed that there are still huge gaps that need to be interlinked to enjoy the benefits from true Digital Health Ecosystem.

Digital Health Ecosystem needs a federated holistic approach and cannot be just few solutions here and there in silos. The challenges exist even replicating such digital health models in developing and underdeveloped countries because the overall digital infrastructure of such countries is still very poor.

In digital health, there are many areas like m-Health for delivering healthcare services and information through mobile devices. Digital and Precision Medicine is essentially tailoring the medical practices according to the needs of individual patients. Quantified Self is a term used for monitoring and predicting an individual's health on the basis of the health parameter data gathered from wearable and other devices and recommend lifestyle and dietary changes, create systemic plans, bring in workout regime to achieve some health-related milestones and targets like weight loss, control hypertension or diabetes, etc. Telemedicine for delivering healthcare remotely using digital technologies, and many more.

Modern digital health services cover a wide spectrum of technologies and approaches, including gamification, implementing mobile technologies, IoT, sensors, different electronic devices, robotics, social media, analytics, data visualization and predictions, 3D printing or bio-printing, blockchain, AR/VR, big data and of course AI and machine learning. The list is very long and newer cutting-edge innovations like quantum computing is also now getting appended in the same list.

The core focus of digital healthcare is proactive and predictive rather than reactive with aggressive treatment plan for ailments and that's a huge paradigm shift from traditional approach of sick care. Personal wearable technologies are coming in full force in the golden era of digital healthcare. Now, wearable health monitoring systems will flourish in a big way and almost all vital body parameters will be available in our mobile devices. With the advent of NewGen sensors powered with AI the field of wearables and personal technologies will get a great boost. Telemedicine, home diagnosis, remote care, retail, and insurance are already getting integrated with the digital health ecosystem. Keeping connected health infrastructure as the backbone and running many varieties of predictive analytics on health parameters can essentially revolutionize the emerging field of predictive health.

Rendering different healthcare services on mobile devices and online consultation, home care, including some critical care at home, and making available medicines, including many medical equipment's and medical kits for home online has already started in India and many parts of the world during this COVID lockdown. In fact, we need such a remote home care ecosystem in parallel with traditional hospital care that has become very essential during crisis situations like pandemic, natural calamity, or war. This can result in drastic reduction in hospital admission rate and thus prevent hospital systems from being overwhelmed during such a crisis. Health social networks are also growing popularity, such as networks provide opportunity to patients to seek advice, suggestions from other similar patients and compare medications, diet, and lifestyle changes, etc. It can also sometimes help getting emotional support from such health social network groups.

Again, technology invasion in healthcare is going to be tremendous in the post COVID era because many people started contemplating that healthcare in its core has somehow been disregarded when we were busy with other technological revolutions. Cutting edge technologies like genetic engineering, artificial intelligence, and even quantum computing has started invading many areas in a big way. Also, healthcare e-commerce has already started booming and has the potential to leapfrog other forms of traditional commerce. Similarly, Bio-Printing of human organs is going to revolutionize the organ transplantation space in near future. Even cars today are becoming point-of-care, and many high-end cars are already equipped with sensory systems in seat belts, steering wheels, and other parts of the car that can sense whether you are very tired during driving, your heartbeat rate is going abnormal, or abnormality in any other vital body parameters can be detected and can immediately alert you and your healthcare provider. It can also guide you through steps and remedial actions which can essentially save your life.

Many experts also realize today that healthcare and medicine industry need light in terms of bringing transparency and openness, especially in the developing countries and technology intervention at large scale. In that way, digital healthcare is going to radically change the dirty way of market expansion and some nasty competition among the drug and medicine companies, healthcare providers, and hospitals by completely ignoring the ethics and the human life element involved in this field. Digital healthcare is going to bring enormous transparency for the patients where there is a huge gap today.

Also, cross-border healthcare or borderless healthcare a long pending dream and digital healthcare revolution is going to transcend the geographical boundaries of different countries and bring healthcare anywhere anytime in true sense. Collaboration among different countries in the field of research in the different verticals of medical science keeping aside geographical and political disparities can bring an immense momentum in this revolution.

The regulatory bodies of different countries will play a major role in this digital healthcare revolution because only if they bring in a forward-thinking conductive environment for the innovators, then only things will move fast. The traditional bureaucratic mentality of the regulators and the governments can slow down the entire process and create frustration among the startups and innovators.

Data privacy is a major challenge and there is a need of a right robust framework to deal with the security, privacy, and sharing of health data related to various health parameters, diagnostic reports, medical history, hospitalization details, treatments undergo, doctors' prescriptions, different types of bills, insurance records, etc. to leverage those to build a better digital health ecosystem.

Surprisingly, most of the innovations that are happening today in the field of healthcare and medicine are been done not by pure healthcare professionals, researchers, or doctors, rather professionals and innovators from other fields like IT, robotics, AI, and people from the fields of applied physics, chemical science and genetics, etc. That clearly indicates that in this century, you need not have to be a qualified healthcare professional or a doctor to participate in this revolution; rather you can be from any field if you are passionate and with a mentality and willingness to innovate.

CHAPTER 5
Quantum Computing in Banking and Finance

Banking and finance is a data-intensive business and many of the crucial decisions demand real-time data insights and predictions. The challenge with the classical computing approach with the huge amount data generated at a super-fast speed is never real time and mostly postmortem. With quantum computing not only those can easily be absolute real-time but also will open far more possibilities.

Some complex derivatives are path-dependent; evaluating innumerous paths used to be computationally very expensive and difficult to understand their interdependence, hence can never be calculated near-real-time with classic computers but quantum computers can easily compute those in real time with the parallelism it provides. This will revolutionize financial market study and prediction of stocks and in the areas of crypto currencies.

IDC Financial Insights recently announced a two-part series that explores the world of quantum computing in the context of banking. They are examining the potential real-world use cases being studied and used by banks worldwide, where certain types of quantum computers will influence the industry's further transformation.

Banks and other financial firms are focusing on using the quantum computing technology to manage and simulate investment portfolios. In some cases, the initial financial services are used for real-time analysis of investment portfolios, such as asset allocation and risk management.

Because quantum computers can theoretically process huge amount of data so quickly, financial firms will be able to analyze the best investment options for portfolios almost immediately and quickly and take a large amount into account for important calculations such as cryptography and cybersecurity. In finance and economics, quantum computing could lead to a range of applications, such as analyzing large areas of heterogeneous data to make financial predictions and understand economic phenomena. Quantum computing which has shown promise in financial services, is a solution to complex problems, for example, in the analysis of financial markets and the management of asset allocation and risk management. All these applications of quantum computers in finance and banking offer a potential value to the financial sector and other industries, especially those with high complexity.

According to Deltec Bank of the Bahamas, the challenge for the banking sector is to maximize the small operational window offered by quantum computers. Maintaining and operating these programs is expensive, so only the largest financial institutions can be involved in quantum computing research and compete for the upper hand in this emerging technology until quantum computing services becomes widespread and economically viable.

Banks and hedge funds think that quantum computing could help them reduce the risk that lurks in their investment portfolios. JPMorgan is already exploring the use of quantum computers to figure out how to streamline its investment and risk management systems. Banks and financial institutions can gain more value from big data by developing algorithms that build on the power of quantum computing.

The current work is largely exploratory and small demonstrations or proof of concepts are being developed to explore how quantum computing systems could serve financial institutions. Goldman Sachs and JPMorgan Chase expect to use quantum computers in their businesses in real time in the next few years.

Standard Chartered, meanwhile, is the latest bank to commit to research into quantum computers as part of an academic partnership. The three-year program will build, operate, and build the first quantum computer in the UK, make it available to banks and other financial institutions, and drive the development of the world's first super-powerful quantum computer. The partnership is already actively developing what is called the **quantum computing system for financial services** (QCS) and will use it to address the security challenges posed by a super-powerful quantum computer. It could be a big step forward for the future of banking and finance, as well as other sectors such as health care:

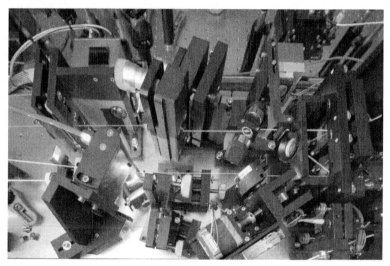

Figure 5.1: *Diagram Source: Banking and Finance*

As per some experts, within five years, companies around the world will have full access to quantum computing as a service and will benefit from a range of benefits, including faster, more efficient, and more secure computing. Quantum computing is developing rapidly and, as a new technology emerging will give companies a competitive advantage as they learn how to use it first. Due to the growing interest in quantum computers, it is believed that there will be sufficient supply of quantum computing talent to meet the demand.

Many industries in the UK's central economy are ready to benefit from quantum computers, including finance, energy, and pharmaceuticals. Some of the world's largest companies, including IBM, IBM Research, Microsoft, Google, Apple, and Microsoft, have already begun to invest in the Quantum Computing technology. While quantum computing is not yet available in prime time, established and newly established quantum computing companies are already merging to gain a competitive advantage.

CHAPTER 6
Quantum Computing in Drug Discovery and Research

Scientist from different universities and advanced research institutes worldwide were always looking for some computational device which are far superior to classic computers, probably more than a supercomputer to better understand genetics of different organisms and various diseases that could led to effective drug discovery or treatment of diseases. With the arrival of Quantum Computers, even at a very nascent state researchers are now tapping into the potential of a quantum computer to understand genetic of diseases and discovery of different drugs in a better way.

According to the study, Polarisqb, a leading drug research company, wants to accelerate the process of drug discovery from 5 years to 4 months using a combination of artificial intelligence and quantum computer technology. By enabling researchers to develop new treatments for a range of diseases, quantum computing will help bring new drugs into trials faster and improve the safety of these trials. Ultimately, it can achieve better results in terms of drug safety and efficacy than existing medicines. This allows them to search for new ways to develop personalized and precision medicines without side effects.

At this stage, we can only refer to these experiments and imagine how quantum computing could improve the clinical imaging, diagnosis, and treatment of the diseases. Nevertheless, recent advances show that quantum computers could eventually enable researchers to better understand known molecules and their interactions, and potentially discover new drugs and materials.

Innovators and researchers working on quantum applications in drug development are already making huge advancements in the pharmaceutical industry. There are several young companies that are looking at the computational boost and predicted accuracy that quantum computing technology could provide in the field of medicine.

It was announced that Schrodinger, a drug discovery and materials design company was working with AstraZeneca to incorporate molecular modeling into drug discovery work. The startup aims to enable the use of quantum computers in drug development in the field of drug research.

Quantum computer-aided algorithms will prove themselves in the field of molecular modeling and drug discovery, but the algorithm can also be exported and imported back into classical computer systems. Investing in partnerships dedicated to building tailored solutions to address the key challenges of drug discovery is an effective way to gain a foothold in the emerging quantum computing ecosystem.

Also, Entropica Lab's software applications focuses on healthcare, drug development, and agricultural technology, giving genome researchers access to the world's most advanced machine learning and quantum algorithms, enabling them to refine and streamline their research faster and more efficiently. New tools, methods, and computer-aided discoveries can be driven through this next generation of research in medicine, health care, agriculture, and other fields.

Research works in the field of chemistry is among the first in terms of adoption and use of quantum computers, which allows the development of new approaches to drug discovery and drug development, as well as the use of quantum computers in other areas. Big data and machine learning are also key elements in the future of advanced research in health care and medicine.

It is therefore essential to understand the impact that quantum computing technology could have on the pharmaceutical industry if we are to ensure that we help discover cures for tenacious diseases such as cancer and Alzheimer's and ensure that the benefits are fairly distributed across the globe.

Drug discovery is one area where quantum computing technology is playing a disruptive role, and the same has already been reflected in the field. The other three major areas that will benefit from quantum computers are predicted to be artificial intelligence, finance, and pharmaceutical research. General advances in quantum computing will help in bringing the benefits to these industries earlier.

Researchers in other fields and IT leaders will be able to push forward joint efforts in the run-up to the competition, as soon as quantum services are ready for their use. A wide range of quantum services and capabilities in the form of specialized and standardized quantum algorithms will be available via cloud soon.

Qulab, a pharmaceutical company, is able to take a leading role in this field of pharmaceutical research. Research suggests that by using quantum computers in drug discovery, a quantum computer could model and test new drugs in real time, effectively reducing the cost of novel drug research and development; also shortened time to improve results in Silico simulation, a growing practice of searching for new molecules on the computer, rather than in a test tube.

Targeted treatments, such as radiotherapy, depend upon the ability to rapidly model and simulate complex scenarios to deliver the optimal treatment. In the future, quantum simulations will enable rapid designer drug testing by accounting for every possible protein-to-drug combination.

Misfolded proteins can cause diseases like Alzheimer's and Parkinson's, and researchers testing new treatments must learn which drugs cause reactions for each protein through the use of random computer modeling. Note that producing energy efficient fertilizer is just one of the many ways we can solve big problems with the ability to accurately simulate molecular behavior.

With quantum computing, medical professionals can open a new chapter in drug prescription outcomes by tailoring each treatment to meet the exact requirements of each individual called personalized or precision medicine.

It will also help drug companies to deliver new molecules and therapies to market faster by streamlining the discovery process and enabling quantum energy calculations for molecules as predicted in the *Pistoia Alliance's* 2030 vision report. Pistoia Alliance is a nonprofit alliance working to lower barriers to innovation in life science and healthcare RandD.

The power of quantum computing will enable researchers and healthcare professionals to discover, pioneer, and deliver more precise and more personalized diagnoses, treatments, and medications.

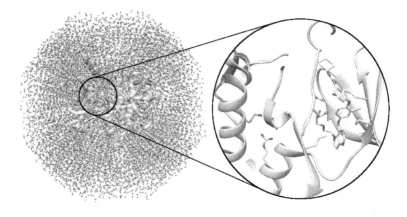

Figure 6.1: *Diagram (Source: profacgen.com)*

Quantum computing is going to boost even CRISPR, a revolutionary gene editing technology that has advanced so rapidly that the Salk Institute for Biological Research, USA had designed a very advanced version of the CRISPR - Cas9 system. CRISPR technology has enabled a simple and affordable method of manipulating and editing DNA that has radically changed the ambitions of synthetic biologists. Researchers *Richard Li, Rosa Di Felice, Remo Rohs,* and *Daniel Lidar* have demonstrated how a quantum processor could be used as a predictive tool to assess a fundamental process in biology, the binding of gene regulatory proteins to the genome.

Genome sequencing creates a lot of data such that a representation of a person's whole DNA strand requires massive computational power and storage capacity. Also, genome researchers have always been annoyed about the security of transferring large-scale genome sequence data; they sometimes physically transport hard disks in locked security boxes, which is problematic in terms of cost and time.

Companies are rapidly bringing down the cost and resources needed to sequence the human genome; however, a quantum computer would make the way genomes are sequenced more efficient and easier to scale globally. A quantum computer could assemble and sort through all possible gene variants at the same time and instantly find all nucleotide pairs, making the whole process of genome sequencing exponentially shorter.

Researchers at the University of Virginia School of Medicine say they are tapping into the potential of quantum computers to help understand genetic diseases.

Scientists from the University have built an algorithm that may throw crucial light on genetic diseases, as well as help physicians and medical experts to rapidly diagnose them.

CHAPTER 7
Quantum Computing in Aviation, Travel, and Logistics

While the next big computer race is already underway, some of the biggest technology companies, including Google, Microsoft, IBM, and few others are already exploring their quantum computing technology in various avenues. Quantum computers can be used to create a new generation of very powerful, low-cost computing ecosystem that will cater to the demand of parallel computation. In addition to many other potential benefits, quantum computing technology will bring great advancements to the aviation industry. Airline companies like Airbus is exploring this technology that leverages the ability to deliver optimization of route and plans. There are already a few applications of quantum computers in development that can support the aircraft on the ground and on the sky.

Airbus Ventures invested in quantum computing startup QC-Ware, which built a quantum computing cloud platform. Boeing, the world's largest aerospace company has become one of the most active players in exploring the potential of quantum computers for the design of different critical components of its aircraft.

Quantum computing could also have an impact on reducing emissions in the aviation industry and speed up the process of introducing new aircrafts, due to increased fuel efficiency and sustainability. This includes the development of new materials such as ultra-durable materials that help aircrafts enter the skies.

The aim is to produce ultra-durable material research using quantum computing, and it involves a variety of fields, including materials science, materials engineering, aerospace, computer science, and advanced manufacturing. Quantum computers promise to enable such advances by combining the special properties of quantum physics with computer science to achieve computing power and parallelism that is exponentially more powerful than conventional computers.

Airbus Group, NASA and *Lookheed Martin* have invested heavily to explore the potential applications of quantum computing technology in aviation and space science. In addition to this, researchers are also targeting photonics which will dominate this sector as well as other areas of the aviation industry such as energy storage and data analysis. Quantum computers based on photons will have many advantages over those based on electrons. Photon based quantum computers going to revolutionized not only aviation and travel industry but all other industries.

Honeywell brings its expertise in quantum computing and its application to the aerospace logistics industry as well as in photonics. The Honeywell team is working on several quantum projects and rendering those cloud-based quantum computing services. This includes the simulation and execution of programs on quantum-photonic hardware.

Also, Microsoft's quantum network partners include several other quantum-oriented technical institutions, including the University of California, San Francisco, and the US Department of Energy. The Quantum Laboratory for Artificial Intelligence is to pioneer how quantum computing technology could help in the development of **artificial intelligence (AI)** and artificial neural networks.

The state-of-the-art control electronics are being developed for the quantum computer, and the possibility of linking high-level quantum algorithms with physical Qubit implementations is now offered. The potential of quantum computers for simulating quantum mechanics is equally transformative in chemistry. There are several ways in which it can be used in a variety of industries, including finance, logistics, and transport.

D-Wave Systems, a well-known company in the field of Quantum along with Lockheed Martin, known for developing military and commercial aircrafts have created the world's first quantum computer unit for the control electronics of its F-35 **Joint Strike Fighter** (**JSF**). At the same time, it has also set up a quantum computing unit at its headquarters in Palo Alto, California, to be used in its next-generation fighter jet, the F / A-18E / F Super Hornet.

Quantum computing is already transforming transport, logistics, utilities, and telecommunications. Quantum computing is a revolutionary technology that has a huge potential to transform the transport sector. Volkswagen is one of the first companies to realize its potential. Accelerating the development of quantum computing Volkswagen is supporting the development of a wide range of quantum applications, from transportation and logistics to energy storage, and communications.

India also wants to develop its native quantum computing capabilities that will help it advance research in different areas, including the travel and logistics industry. Tata Institute of Fundamental Research is a pioneer and working on developing its indigenous quantum processor.

Quantum computers have the potential to explore such problems more efficiently and comprehensively than traditional computers and offer advantages over emerging AI-based approaches. India also plans to hire a number of scientists and engineers from different universities and companies abroad who can build quantum computers and then find commercial applications for them in different areas. Few Indian IT companies are also exploring what to do when they see that the more experimental area of the quantum computing system can extract better solutions faster than the classic equivalent.

Quantum computing could have an impact on reducing emissions in the aviation industry, due to increased fuel efficiency and the acceleration of the process of bringing new aircrafts into the skies. The aviation industry will be powered by high energy storage with high energy density and will be CO_2-free if flights become emission-free someday.

Although the technology is still a new development, there are already some applications for quantum computer systems that support the flight process. Technologies to help aircrafts enter the skies include the use of high-energy storage and quantum computers, and the development of new technologies such as superconductors that transport aircraft data and many more. There are a number of other applications of quantum computed auxiliary aircraft on the ground, and some of them include their use in the maintenance and servicing of aircrafts on the ground and aircrafts in flight.

CHAPTER 8
Quantum Computing in Crypto and Security

While the next big computer race is already underway, some of the biggest technology companies, including Google, Microsoft, IBM, and few others are already exploring their quantum computing technology in various avenues. Quantum computers can be used to create a new generation of very powerful, low-cost computing ecosystem that will cater to the demands of parallel computation.

We will not go into the fundamentals of cryptography and quantum properties like superposition and interference or *"Shor's Algorithm"* in this article. We would rather briefly discuss the challenges that are emerging in the conventional cryptographic and security arena as quantum computers are adding up more qubits onto it and becoming more powerful.

Cryptographers have been working for years to prepare for the possible arrival of quantum computers by developing so called quantum-secure encryption methods. Fearful about the fact that quantum breakthroughs are imminent and threaten the sanctity of known encryption algorithms, cryptographers were seeking to develop quantum-resistant crypto that can withstand the intervention of quantum computers.

It all started with the assumption that classical computers will never be powerful enough to crack AES and RAS. But all assumptions came under threat when quantum computers came into picture. Although AES-256 symmetric keys are believed to be quantum resistant, but if the quantum algorithm can run on a large-scale quantum computer, it will be capable of cracking even such strong encryptions to the point where all your encrypted data at rest as well as transit are at risk. Of course, quantum computers will have to add more qubits onto itself before it can break such a fairly complex encryption. But that's just a matter of time because the speed with which it is advancing, the day is not far when it will be able to crack almost every encryption that is built using conventional methods.

Good news is, given the work already underway, researchers have started developing quantum secure cryptography before large quantum computers with a large number of qubits become available to break RSA. Quantum computers are unlikely to pose a practical threat to symmetric cryptography and asymmetric cryptography at least for some years. The reason being the quantum behavior of subatomic particles qubits still do not remain stable for long enough. The "Shor Algorithm" used by a quantum computer with enough stable qubits to break through today's public-key cryptography still have some time, so there is no risk at least for now. However, the asymmetry of cryptography like RSA, on which we rely today, could be broken by the quantum computers.

Also called "*quantum-resistant*" or "*post-quantum*"; the next generation of cryptography is designed to withstand quantum computers are being developed in collaboration with the University of California, Berkeley, and the National Institute of Standards and Technology (NIST) in the United States.

We will have to look at the post-quantum cryptography algorithm, which claims to be able to protect data even from the capabilities of quantum computers, called quantum attack. This type of mechanism is called Quantum secure cryptography.

The use of quantum cryptography now not only provides immediate protection for your data, but also secures high-quality data and ensures that data with long shelf life is protected against future attacks. It is important that a protocol with information-theoretical security means that security is not based on arithmetical assumptions and remains secure. In addition, the key management systems and protocols used are also inherently protected against attacks by quantum computers.

Faced with this looming threat, IT decision-makers should consider post-quantum cryptography, where a secure attack by a quantum computer would take place in the critical IT systems tomorrow. Today's public key cryptography has proven to be safe from mathematical attacks but not from quantum computers.

The good side is harnessing quantum computing and AI, and it's going to bring very exciting opportunities in almost every field and industry.

With the massive parallelism of quantum computing, it brings to the table combined with the cognitive element of AI, many possibilities to solve critical problems that we used to dismiss as unsolvable till now.

CHAPTER 9
Quantum Computing in Space Exploration, Astronomical, and Weather Studies

Researchers trying to build the next generation of quantum computers are pushing the boundaries of what can be achieved with the current experimental technology. The Quantum Science Center, led by the Oak Ridge National Lab is exploring quantum computers and developing quantum sensors that could lead to new applications in space research, astronomy, and weather forecasting. Researchers are working on a range of quantum computer algorithms optimized for high-performance computing, quantum data processing, and quantum information processing. This is used to address issues that traditional supercomputers cannot handle, such as data mining, data storage, and data analysis in real-time when the size is humongous.

Quantum computing is still an evolving field, and universities and basic research laboratories contribute the most on its progress, but the main players working on quantum computing still include Google, IBM and NASA. When large companies like Google or NASA are involved in a new cutting-edge technology, we do not have to wait long for a breakthrough. The Institute of Quantum Information Science and Technology of the Chinese Academy of Sciences is part of a larger effort to significantly advance research in Qi and quantum technology that has been underway since 2017.

Also, the University of Strathclyde researchers are partners in a project which will use cutting-edge quantum technologies to transform understanding of the universe and answer key questions on the nature of dark matter. The international Quantum Interferometry (QI) collaboration aims to search for dark matter and for quantum aspects of space-time with quantum technologies.

From providing geolocation information for weapons systems to other research pipelines, including studying space weather and black holes, investment in space is seen as a means to spur innovation. NASA is also deploying the technology for next-generation space missions, with quantum computers making mission plans more efficient and supporting research into cutting-edge materials and the development of new technologies for space exploration.

A quantum computer can detect more exoplanets, help quickly identify those with the greatest potential for life, and gather more data from the telescope's perspective. A quantum computer can detect and quickly help other exoplanets, quickly locate them, and identify those with the greatest potential for harboring life. A quantum computer can detect more exoplanets and collect more of this data, thus allowing telescopes to see them. The quantum computer was able to quickly discover them and quickly identify the one that has most of these potentials for harbingers of life. Quantum computing technology can change the world and change how our work is to accelerate space exploration.

CHAPTER 10
Quantum Computing for Solving Complex Optimization Problems

Experts agree that quantum computers have the potential to solve the hardest optimization problem utilizing technique like Quantum Annealing. Quantum Annealing is a metaheuristic for finding the global minimum of a given objective function over a given set of candidate solutions, by a process using quantum fluctuations. Quantum computers use the probability laws of quantum physics to process data and perform calculations in a novel way. Quantum computers, for example, can perform real-time calculations to solve incredibly complex problems.

They are also ideal for solving complex optimization tasks and for quick searching for unsorted data.

In banking and finance, some complex derivatives are path dependent. Evaluating numerous paths used to be computationally very expensive and difficult to understand. Hence, they can never be calculated near-real-time with classical computers, but quantum computers can easily compute those in real-time. This is revolutionizing the financial market study and prediction of stocks and cryptocurrencies.

Quantum annealing can be used to solve similar optimization problems in transportation and logistics, aviation, or any other resource optimization like manufacturing inventory, advertising, etc. for that matter. The optimization problem is usually formulated as a minimization problem, where one tries to minimize errors depending on the solution and the optimal solution has minimal errors. D-waves solve an optimization problem and achieve the best solution by quantum annealing.

For a quantum computer to solve these major challenges, we need to understand how to formulate the problem and how it interacts with classical computers in a hybrid model. Quantum annealing is a method to solve the problem to find a way to find the optimal solution to a complex optimization problem with a large number of possible solutions. Approximate optimization is the process of finding approximate solutions to optimization problems, which is often difficult. Simulating an annealing algorithm is a useful method for solving problems where the fastest heuristic solution is an exact one, which takes too long to solve.

Quantum computers are best known for solving optimization problems across different industries. Some examples – Volkswagen uses D-Wave quantum services for traffic flow optimization and acoustic horn shape optimization. DENSO, Japan uses it for manufacturing process optimization. Recruit Communications, Japan uses for Internet advertising optimization. DLR Germany for air traffic route optimization. Similarly, Nomura Securities for financial portfolio optimization and British Telecom for cell phone network optimization.

Various social systems, including communication, transport, and social networks, require complex combinatorial optimization problems to be solved. As the complexity and amount of data increases, different optimization techniques must be used to solve these optimization problems. This is expected to lead to the development of quantum computers that can be used to solve complex problems, such as the problem of a traveling salesman with a large number of possible solutions and a complex social network.

We have seen that quantum computers can very efficiently calculate approximate gradients of convex functions. The answer to this question gives us the opportunity to offer a quantum computer solution to the problem of complex optimization problems in computer vision and computer graphics.

CHAPTER 11
Quantum Computing in Chemistry, Chemical Research, and Agriculture

One of the major implementations of Quantum Computing Technology is in the field of chemical research, study of different molecules, and biochemistry. Also, researchers have developed a quantum chemical simulation benchmark to evaluate the performance of quantum devices and to guide the development and application of future quantum computers in chemical research and other fields.

Although quantum computing is one of the hottest topics in science today, the instructions and algorithms for quantum computers have still sometime to go to become economically viable in different areas of business. The researchers were the first to include a quantum computer in the modeling of chemical reactions and their Hartree-Fock calculations. **Hartree–Fock (HF)** method is a method of approximation for the determination of the wave function and the energy of a quantum many-body system in a stationary state.

Quantum chemistry is the area of computational chemistry that tries to understand how molecules react with one another, what their energies are, and how atoms move around in a chemical reaction. A new catalyst is something that even the largest computers today are struggling to realize. But quantum computers will be able to do it perfectly. Although quantum computers are still maturing to get that desired accuracy, but we will get that accuracy soon. For example, the process of converting nitrogen into ammonia for fertilizers is a very energy-intensive reaction. And how it can be achieved at scale will enable us to produce enough food for a global population. A quantum computer should take molecular simulations to the next level by accurately and quickly predicting the results of complex chemical reactions. It would be able to quickly analyze chemical catalytic processes and develop optimal catalyst combinations for ammonia production.

Catalysis is a perfect candidate for Quantum computing in chemistry. Our most powerful classical computers are limited in the chemical modeling. They can't unlock what solutions could be develop; for example, to address sustainability. What if we were able to model more complex molecules and reactions efficiently and what if we are able to do that on a scalable quantum computer.

The science of catalysis is trying to understand how to works and use the chemical knowledge to be able to design better ways to carry out the conversion. With catalysis, scientists really want to improve that efficiency and have less dependence on our natural resources. At this moment, due to the limitations of a number of qubits, there is no quantum algorithm that can predict chemical reactions with a significant number of qubits in a quantum computer at scale, but there are some that are capable of doing so with smaller numbers. There are no practical quantum algorithms that make it possible to determine the predicted chemical reaction paths considering post-Hartree jib calculations. However, there are some that they have been able to put into practice in quantum computers with a considerable number of quantities.

Another example is quantum chemical dynamics; a problem that is important for a variety of applications such as artificial photosynthesis. As far as possible applications are concerned, the field of chemistry is expected to be the first to use quantum computers to calculate complex chemical reactions, such as the synthesis of chemical compounds. Researchers at **Oklahoma City University (OCU)** have already made progress in implementing a new quantum algorithm for generating certain waves, known as **configuration state functions (CSFs)**, with polynomial computing time between 20163 and 20184, and have addressed a number of problems in chemistry and chemical research in general, as well as in the application of quantum chemistry to a variety of biological systems. They have also addressed the quantum state function of a chemical reaction in a quantum computer system, in particular with regard to the creation of new chemical molecules, such as a reaction between two different types of organic molecules in an organic chemical system (for example hydrochloric acid and nitric acid) and have already made progress in the implementation of the polynomial computing.

As quantum computers become more powerful, these computers will enable chemists to solve problems that cannot be solved by today's classic computers, even supercomputers. But, with the advancement of quantum computing technology, it is now clear that these devices will solve it most effectively. Quantum physics, quantum biology, and other areas of science and technology, such as computer vision and quantum information processing will also start using quantum computers, but quantum chemistry is a very promising field of research.

CHAPTER 12
Quantum Computing in Artificial Intelligence and Machine Learning

Quantum computers have the potential to give artificial intelligence a big boost, according to a series of studies. Quantum computing can be used to optimize classic machine learning algorithms and create optimized algorithms. One promising idea currently being studied by leading IT companies such as Google, Microsoft, and IBM Research is to harness the potential of the quantum computing systems to optimize machine learning.

The studies described suggest that machine learning can be redirected to control brittle quantum devices and quantum computers and can help design and improve varying algorithms. At the same time, the entire scientific community is relying on the first publication in Quantum Machine Intelligence.

Technically, quantum machine intelligence is a problem in artificial intelligence and machine learning the solution of algorithms for the application of quantum computer technology in artificial intelligence. TFQ is a research group for quantum computing technology at the University of California, Berkeley, which is one of the world's largest research institutes in the field of artificial intelligence and machine learning.

By using superposition and entanglement, computers can perform quantum operations that are difficult to emulate on the scale of classical computers. Quantum computer systems rely on the properties of quantum mechanics to calculate problems that would be unattainable with a classical computer. It contributes to the effectiveness of the process by using quantum computer algorithms to execute machine learning. This can be achieved by quickly presenting an optimal solution, which is determined by the weights of an artificial neural network.

In business, quantum computers enable rapid analysis and integration of large data sets, which in turn improves and transforms machine learning and artificial intelligence capabilities. The MIT Technology Report agrees that a quantum computer will be particularly suited to account for large numbers, solve complex optimization problems, and execute machine-learning algorithms.

With quantum computers, this could mean that future applications in quantum simulation space will increasingly benefit. Big data research and machine learning are likely to be among the areas that make the most progress in terms quantum computers.

ML - based analysis solutions require the aggregation and analysis of data to train them to learn the observed behavior in the real world. Artificial intelligence will likely require quantum computing technology to make significant progress towards **Artificial General Intelligence (AGI)**.

Quantum computing and artificial intelligence are transformative technologies and have a significant impact on the development of machine learning algorithms for artificial intelligence that can harness the power of quantum computation to deliver real-time results.

IBM is trying to combine Watson's efforts with quantum computers to create precise, human-like AI. Future machine learning programs will require the computing power of quantum computation to deal with complexity while simultaneously delivering real-time results. IBM believes this, suggesting that by 2025, quantum computing technology will transform machine learning.

TensorFlow Quantum will greatly facilitate new ways to combine Tensor Flow's classic machine learning capabilities with the new capabilities of the quantum computing system, such as Google's Sycamore chip, which recently reached the quantum supremacy standard. Machine learning challenges are particularly suitable for quantum computing, but the promise is that quantum computers will enable the development of new, faster, more powerful, and efficient quantum machines that will improve and transform both machine learning and artificial intelligence capabilities. Other applications of quantum technology, particularly data analysis, could even prove crucial in the future.

We have already seen that quantum computing would theoretically be able to significantly increase the execution speed of machine learning. This groundbreaking scenario was spearheaded by increasingly sophisticated results showing how quantum computers can solve artificial intelligence problems faster than their classical counterparts.

There is also a machine learning algorithm known as Deep Amplification Learning, which has been applied to quantum computing. It is also the first application in the real world in the field of artificial intelligence research powered with Quantum Computing.

Quantum computing and quantum machine learning are two of the most promising areas of research in the field of computer science and technology. The release of a quantum machine learning tool that can help scientists and developers quickly develop quantum neural network models and deliver advanced quantum computing applications.

TensorFlow Quantum (TFQ) provides a framework for combining natural and artificial quantum systems and machine learning models to control them. This new framework offers quantum computer researchers and learners a new way to bring the power and possibilities of machine learning into the realm of quantum computing.

The MIT Technology Report agrees that quantum computers will be particularly suited to account for large numbers, solve complex optimization problems, and execute machine learning algorithms. So, companies can quickly analyze and integrate large data sets, which in turn improve and transform machine learning and artificial intelligence capabilities.

There are interfaces in which quantum computers use machine learning algorithms and traditional machine learning methods to evaluate them. For example, it can be found out whether a quantum computer can accelerate the time it takes to train and evaluate a machine learning model. We have a number of machine learning algorithms in artificial intelligence that can harness the power of the quantum computing system to deliver real-time results.

For example, quantum-inspired and generalized learning ideas stand out in computer vision and machine intelligence but are ultimately only a small part of a much larger, more complex field.

Quantum machine learning enables scientists to adopt classical ML algorithms and translate them into quantum circuits so that they can run efficiently on a quantum computer.

Big data and machine learning are likely to be one of the most important advanced fields in quantum computing in the near future. Quantum computers allow a much more efficient use of quantum computers than GPUs in the past. With quantum computation, this could mean that future applications in the quantum simulation space will increasingly benefit from quantum algorithms such as deep learning, deep neural networks, and quantum simulations.

Quantum parallelization and quantum-associative memory have been used to solve many of the problems in machine learning and AI, and they have proven to accelerate computation. One area of particular interest for the future of AI is the use of **quantum neural networks (QNN)**, a type of artificial neural network. These functions will help machine-learned algorithms to calculate with less computing time.

CHAPTER 13

Quantum Computing for Optimizing Big Data

With regard to big data, quantum computing will enable companies to capture a large amount of data and optimize them for the optimal use and valuable insights with great speed. Quantum computing comes with a great promise for the optimization of a large amount of data and the most complicated data problems in connection with big data and their optimal processing and use.

Quantum computers can help to ease machine learning problems; for example, there is a quantum interpretation of SVM kernel tricks that can help reduce calculations to a specific dimension and allow the optimization of a large amount of data and their optimal use, thus allowing to reduce calculations for a particular dimension and allowing the splitting of these high-dimensional datasets into more manageable ones. As we know, the most appropriate applications of quantum computers are probably those that require a large number of calculations, such as large data sets, QC can be of great help to ease these problems.

Artificial intelligence could analyze big data at a granular level, and powerful quantum processors would be able to process these massive datasets with the parallel processing capability. Together AI and QC can analyze large data sets at a granular level; a powerful quantum processor could process massive data sets and handle them at granularity level.

The capabilities of quantum computing help build more scalable prediction models that can handle a huge amount of data and insert as many variables into the equation as possible without slowing down essential processes. Quantum computer systems reduce the most difficult optimization problems to a number of operations. It is also ideal for solving complex optimization tasks and performing quick searches for unsorted data. This could allow the development of more efficient algorithms for analyzing a large amount of data.

Addressing the processing capability and storage capacity challenges of big data is not simply a question of building more storage and adding more nodes in many cases because the problem may demand for some parallelism and optimization.

It is about changing the computer architecture, which requires a new approach to big data, not only in terms of storage capacity, but also in terms of computing power and parallelism.

The goal is to use the quantum computer to create new classifiers that can generate maps with more complex data. Quantum computer systems are expected to be able to search very large, unsorted datasets to detect patterns and anomalies extremely quickly. Quantum computing could work well with machine learning algorithms to detect patterns in a huge dataset, such as whether data clusters are linked to keywords, or whether some of the data is in some way similar. If the quantum computer is sufficiently scaled to process this dataset, this algorithm alone could process unprecedented amounts of data at high speed.

There is a narrow approach to quantum computing, known as quantum glow, in which Qubits are used to accelerate optimization problems. This method, which has worked in limited settings, also makes use of the possibility to scale to the larger quantum computers that are planned for the future. Another approach is accelerating as **Noisy Intermediate-Scale Quantum Computing (NISQ)** machines become more powerful.

Big data is the area that would benefit most from the combination of artificial intelligence and quantum computers. Quantum computing is part of the broader competition for big data, and big data is the area where we would benefit most from a link between artificial intelligence and a quantum computer.

First, quantum computers are capable of solving logistical optimization problems that are the root cause of many challenges in almost all the industries. In particular, the area of quantum computing technology that is most promising for financial services is the optimization of large data sets.

Here is a list of systems and methods that offer optimization services for quantum computing and big data management in a distributed computing environment that can be used for a wide range of applications in bioinformatics, bioengineering, and other fields. Users can perform algorithms and experiments on a quantum computer processor that works on quantum bits (qubits) and can enable systems to efficiently use databases and data stores to search large data lists, shorten response times, and efficiently evaluate a larger amount of data.

Considering that quantum computers are capable of finding and protecting sensitive data and communication, and accurately simulating quantum phenomena and molecular behavior will facilitate the development of industry specific quantum solutions tailored to the needs of a wide range of industries, such as healthcare, healthcare, finance, energy, telecommunications, transport, agriculture, etc.

All systems and processes that require computing time can benefit from quantum computers, and quantum computing resources can be accessed remotely, for example in the cloud. Big data processing and analytics can also be done closer to the user by using a quantum computer and its quantum data storage and processing resources.

Meanwhile, IBM has developed its own quantum experience, which enables engineers and researchers to perform quantum computing in the IBM cloud. The quantum computer playground can efficiently simulate quantum registers of up to 22 qubits, execute Grover Shor algorithms, and incorporate quantum gates into the scripting language itself. This example demonstrates distributed computing using the integration provided with the Big Data Computing Framework. Similar cloud services have been launched by Microsoft, Google, and D-Wave.

One of the most important challenges in analyzing a large amount of complex "*big data*" is the ability to distribute and process them in parallel across multiple nodes.

A distributed quantum computer with nodes connected according to a hypercube graph would be able to emulate any quantum circuit with only a certain amount of overhead. Quantum parallelism allows a single quantum computer to do the work of a distributed system of classical computers and enables techniques that use efficient quantum algorithms. It is also believed to be able to solve complex problems such as the integer factorization underlying RSA encryption much faster than a classical computer.

Chapter 14
Quantum Computing for Simulation of Durable Battery Designs

One of the important applications of quantum computers is in the field of materials science and chemistry. The most promising fact is that quantum computers can perform much more complex calculations than even today's supercomputers can handle.

The hope is that quantum computers can speed up the simulation process by accurately predicting properties of new molecules that can explain their behavior, such as reactivity. Companies such as Daimler and Volkswagen have already invested in the development of such algorithms, which are to run on a quantum computer.

Cambridge Quantum Computing, a developer of quantum-computing algorithms, is working with the German Aerospace Center to investigate how quantum machines can be used to boost the fidelity of battery simulations. The quantum algorithms are being applied to solve partial differential equations, rendering an initial one-dimensional simulation of a lithium-ion battery cell.

The machine learning framework provides the foundation for rendering full-3D battery simulations that can be executed on quantum computers to improve the performance of the Lithium-ion battery, and to check how much energy they can store without compromising on safety.

The research also addresses battery-durability and supply-chain issues such as reducing reliance on lithium used in commercial batteries. Research could also focus on alternative battery materials like plentiful, high-energy zinc.

The 3D battery-simulation models also provide a new use case for emerging quantum-computing platforms, including noisy systems like IBM's Q. Those platforms are being augmented by machine-learning algorithms like Cambridge Quantum's. The combination would lay the foundation for high-resolution, multi-scale simulation models, the partners said, including simulations of entire battery cells.

Researchers at Daimler hope that quantum computers can help them by calculating their fundamental behavior and accurately simulating it. Also, Oak Ridge National Laboratory is focusing on scientific applications spanning the full spectrum of quantum computing technology, from quantum computer design and simulation to battery design.

Mercedes-Benz is exploring quantum computing for simulation of their battery design for the electric vehicles. Mercedes-Benz collaborating with IBM for utilizing IBM Quantum for their research to understand and simulate at molecular level to build more efficient battery design and even search for advanced battery material.

In other words, a quantum computer could transform the field of chemistry and play a central role in materials science research and provide crucial support for the development of new materials, materials science, and materials technologies, as well as the production of advanced materials. The QC could also give a boost to the automotive players as they move into the electric vehicle age, particularly by accelerating research and development of new technologies. We see how quantum computing applications can accelerate the transition to electric cars and autonomous vehicles.

CHAPTER 15
Quantum Computing and Future of Autonomous Vehicles

Autonomous vehicles are undoubtedly the future. These fully automated cars are an astounding wonder that can totally change the way we perceive our lives, especially in terms of transportation and commutation. From mobile retail stores to on-the-move restaurants and gyms, autonomous cars can promise all that and so much more.

But when will they actually grace our roads and gain a permanent place in our lives? This would obviously depend on our preparedness to accept this mind-blowing automobile transformation and the ability to efficiently utilize such top-grade technology without compromising human independence and safety concerns.

Autonomous vehicle manufacturers have promised a blissful and a highly innovative future for the driverless autonomous cars. There has been a lot of speculation regarding the impact of the fully automated cars on the automotive industry worldwide and how these driverless cars can practically transform the world into a futuristic and digitized entity.

According to forecasters, autonomous vehicles can bring forth an altogether new era of economic and technological advancement.

Although fully autonomous vehicles are still in the testing stage, but surely, they are going to grace the roadways in less than a decade. Now, Quantum Computers can enhance the functioning of autonomous vehicles to a great extent. In fact, it will bring a revolution in the field of autonomous vehicles and quality of transportation.

Quantum computers will be a key enabler for the future of artificial intelligence, artificial neural networks, and other advanced technologies such as Robotics and Autonomous Vehicles. Quantum computers will make a major contribution to improve the safety and efficiency of autonomous driving. Quantum computing remains to be seen, but hopefully self-driving technology companies that can leverage quantum cloud capabilities will be able to advance their research and development efforts. In the meantime, companies like Google, Apple, Microsoft, Tesla, Google, and many others are making strides, opening up new opportunities and keeping their cars at the wheel.

This provides technology companies a way forward to develop solutions that automate operations and deliver better results for all.

Companies like Daimler (Mercedes) and Qantas are also exploring how they could potentially use quantum computing along with artificial intelligence, and control autonomous vehicles in the future and speed up its logistics. The two parties are working together to apply quantum computing to research programs for autonomous vehicles. Much of the ongoing learning process for autonomous cars will take place in large data centers that will process enormous amounts of data. Quantum computing applications are run in a hybrid solution, where smaller problems handled by **High Performance Computing (HPCs)** are outsourced to quantum computers and the results are fed back into the HPC flow.

We might be bit away from fully capitalizing on Quantum Computing in some industries, but reports reveal that the automotive and transportation industry is already embracing this emerging technology. The autonomous vehicle industry is one of the various beneficiaries of quantum Computing. Quantum computing can solve the issues of the safety and reliability of autonomous vehicles. Quantum computing will help ease the journey traffic congestion by analyzing data from the sensors inside autonomous vehicles. Thus, ensuring route optimization training to its deep learning algorithm. Quantum computing can be used to train algorithms, while designing autonomous vehicles, to enable better safety and fuel efficiency. There are various areas quantum computing that can provide a boost to automotive players and transition into the autonomous electric vehicle era.

It would also be useful to think about how quantum computers will influence the emergence of real self-driving cars. A quantum computer that can already be used is the quantum glow computer developed by the Canadian company D-Wave Systems. Overall, cloud quantum computing can be used in a variety of ways to help with self-driving cars. Quantum computers can play a major role in the future of self-driving cars and their future applications in autonomous vehicles.

Quantum computing is a cutting-edge technology that could transform the transport sector, and Volkswagen is one of the companies to realize its potential. Meanwhile, OEMs such as Volkswagen and Daimler are working together to deploy QC in their electric vehicle technology. The QC could give a boost to the car players who are moving to the electric vehicle age, and in particular accelerate research and development of new technologies.

VW has announced that it will work with Google to optimize traffic flow and make car batteries more durable. The specialists want to continue the development of traffic optimization, explore the use of quantum computers in the design and implementation of autonomous vehicles, and work on the integration of artificial intelligence and quantum computation in autonomous vehicle systems.

Overall, cloud quantum computers can be used in a variety of ways to help self-driving cars. The quantum computer applications are run as hybrid solutions, in which smaller problems handled by the HPC are outsourced to the quantum computer and the results are fed back into the HPC flow. With huge speed advantages, we could potentially be able to create the revamped AI that can be pushed into driverless fleets sooner.

CHAPTER 16
Quantum Computing in Education and Research

The Julich Supercomputing Centre had teamed up with Google in collaboration with the University of California, Berkeley, and Max Planck Institute for quantum computing. The aim is to develop a qualitative understanding of quantum computing technology and to teach students about quantum in schools, colleges, universities, and research institutes around the world and to the general public. They teach students with little or no experience in quantum computing to write quantum algorithms, understand superconductor physics, and solve quantum chemical problems with Qiskit. Qiskit is an open-source software development kit (SDK) for working with OpenQASM and the IBM Q quantum processors.

Someone who is a novice and wants to learn QC can refer to the series *Quantum Computing in Realities* by MIT which has two main chapters. The first is called *Introduction to Quantum Computing* and the second *Quantum Computing: The Future of Computer Technology in Education and Research*.

In particular, the Quantum Educators program provides professors and students with the latest learning resources designed to help them get started with programming and experimenting with quantum computers. MIT offers courses that introduce the fundamentals of quantum computing technology and its applications in education and research.

MIT was running a **massive online course** (**mooc**) to train quantum intelligence and will help spread knowledge and understanding of quantum computers even to high school students. The newly launched Qiskit Global Summer School, a virtual two-week event, is designed to empower the next generation of quantum developers to write quantum applications themselves.

It is interesting to think about the potential of designing a full course on quantum computing for school and college students, as well as for the next generation of researchers.

Quantum computing UK offers a website with several tutorials that introduce the reader to quantum computing. Michael Nielsen has written an excellent article on quantum computing technology in education and research at the University of California, Berkeley. He also maintains a code repository that allows someone to run programs on a quantum computer. He has also conducted research and published articles and papers on quantum computing algorithms, developed, and launched Katas, a series of computing tasks that classical computer scientists can use to learn quantum computing skills.

Other universities that provide Quantum Computing courses and research opportunities are as follows:

- Harvard University
- Massachusetts Institute of Technology
- National University of Singapore
- Nanyang Technological University
- University of California Berkeley
- University of Sydney
- University of Maryland
- University of Science and Technology of China

In India, the **Ministry of Electronics and Information Technology** (**MeitY**) has introduced the country's first **Quantum Computer**

Simulator (QSim) Toolkit, brought together by the **Indian Institute of Science (IISc)** Bangalore, **Indian Institute of Technology (IIT)** Roorkee, and **Centre for Development of Advanced Computing (C-DAC)**. The project was financed by MeitY and evolved through a multi-institutional approach by the three institutes.

The government of India introduced the **National Mission on Quantum Technologies and Applications (NMQTA)** emphasizing the significance of quantum technology in India. IBM India recently integrated with leading institutions of India to accelerate training and research in quantum computing.

Similarity, **Tata Institute of Fundamental Research (TIFR)** is also doing significant work on quantum research. A list of Indian Universities and institutes providing quantum education are given as follows:

- Indian Institute of Technology

- Indian Institutes of Information Technology

- Indian Institutes of Science Education and Research

- Tata Institute of Fundamental Research

- Indian Statistical Institute

- Calcutta University

CHAPTER 17

How Quantum AI and Will Revolutionize Defense and Warfare?

It has always been witnessed that the defense research organizations of various countries across the globe used to be in the forefront when it comes to adopting cutting-edge technologies. Of course, it was a question of survival and first-mover advantage during the two World Wars, but it continued to be a tradition even after that and countries continued to invest a lot in their technological endeavors in the field of defense research. It is also true that many of the technological innovations and breakthroughs we are enjoying today had happened in the defense research labs at one point and later extended to the industry and academia. So, a powerful quantum computing ecosystem is already in the wish list of the defense research departments of many countries. And why not, in this age of Cyber and Cyborg warfare, quantum computing can play the role of a game changer. Experts believe that quantum computers could make a significant contribution to the future of military equipment and ammunition industries.

This article is NOT intended to showcase the dark side aspects of quantum computing; rather the intension is to highlight the possible applications of this groundbreaking technology.

Defense scientists of many countries are taking a closer look at the impact that Quantum Computing, Quantum Communications, and IoT will have on their national security and defense. It is believed that of the two areas, Quantum Encryption and Quantum Sensors, will have an enormous impact in this field in coming years. Use of quantum computers in communications that can revolutionize Underwater Warfare is of paramount importance in the defense world.

The Quantum Computation and Quantum Communication will also revolutionize *Defense Logistics*. Declining cycle times, increased awareness of the situation, and more efficient communication are just some of the advantages that quantum computation or secure quantum communication will offer in the field of Defense Logistics.

Technologies like Artificial Intelligence, Virtual Reality, Augmented Reality, and Blockchain are already in use to enhance defense capabilities. The future of warfare will be determined by new technologies such as Space-based Internet Infrastructure/backbone and Quantum-based Cryptography, etc. While the use of quantum computing could mean that today's widespread and critical encryption methods will become obsolete, the technology also promises a whole new generation of secure communications. We can expect the use of a quantum cryptography network and a significant increase in the number of fast and secure communication networks in the coming years. Also, one of the most promising applications for quantum computing in military defense is *Lattice-Based* cryptography, which can provide algorithms that are safe against quantum attacks.

Also, accurate navigation that does not require GPS signals is one of the most sought-after skills that would be supported by the quantum computing technology.

Intelligence agencies around the world, in particular, are investigating quantum computing for its possible use as a means of gathering and monitoring vital information. In the future, it could also be used for analysis and data mining and many such things that are very essential as part of intelligence gathering for the agencies. Such agencies in particular are fascinated by the potential of the quantum computing systems to develop secure communications and inertial navigation. Given these strategic applications, there is a strong interest in harnessing the power of quantum mechanics, and governments around the world are investing in this area to preserve and maintain strategic advantages.

Quantum Machine Learning algorithms are likely to be used for a wide range of applications such as GPS navigation and inertial navigation in GPS systems. The US Air Force, Marine, and Lockheed Martin are exploring it in the development of advanced navigation systems and advanced communications systems for the Navy and Marines.

That day is not far when many countries would like their defense departments to have access to the world's most advanced quantum computing technology for many advantages and there has already been a huge investment done on Quantum research by many wealthy nations. USA, China, and few other European countries are already ahead in the race and many others are in the process of developing their indigenous quantum computers. In India, Tata Institute of Fundamental Research is the pioneer in this field and trying to build a 3 Qubit Quantum Computer to demonstrate a unique design and architecture which is indigenously developed by the scientists of TIFR. Once this model is successful, the scientists believe that scaling it to a higher number of Qubits will not be so difficult. They also claim that this design which is an approach of building a quantum processor may have many more advantages than the design and approach used in some of the existing quantum computers. Also, the Indian Government recently declared more than 8000 crores for quantum computing research which is a very good sign for a country like India.

CHAPTER 18

Quantum Computing in Life Science

For decades, theoretical physicists and computer scientists have been collecting evidence that quantum computers will eventually leave the current supercomputers in the dust. Quantum computers will address the need of next-generation quantum algorithms that will enable critical scientific, economic, and social advances. Quantum computing and related quantum technologies represent an exciting new field of research and development that will capture the imagination and harness the ingenuity of scientists and engineers. This should lead to more research into the generation of an errors-tolerant quantum computer that can calculate without limitations. Quantum activated sensors that can harness the exponential power of quantum computing technology to achieve data collection that would have profound implications for our understanding of the world around us, from the environment to the human body to other lives in the planet. Materials scientists and quantum engineers are working to improve the performance of the basic hardware elements of quantum computers.

Quantum computing uses the principles of quantum physics to encode data in several states simultaneously, opening the door to an exponential increase in computing power and parallelism. In addition, the quantum computing technology is expected to provide growth opportunities in the market, and this factor is a major driver of the growth of the global quantum computing market and its applications. Quantum computer systems can perform complex calculations much faster than classical computers.

A wide range of organizations have access to quantum services and functions that can be accessed via the cloud using specialized and standardized quantum algorithms. Quantum software and algorithms are maturing rapidly, making quantum computing a viable alternative or complement to traditional computer systems for a wide range of applications.

Unfortunately, some useful applications of quantum algorithms will likely require large quantum computers that may not be available for few years from now. Classical computers still cannot simulate complex molecules accurately enough, and quantum computing will be able to help. There is some evidence that a quantum computer can help predict the structure of simplified protein models; though it is difficult to determine how much this helps and how long we will have to wait before we have enough qubits in a quantum computer and algorithms to produce meaningful results.

What is fascinating is that even a small quantum computer relatively and a smaller number of qubits can perform calculations and simulations much faster than a supercomputer. Quantum computing technology will make work faster and more methodical, leading to faster and more accurate calculations and more. Quantum computers will be able to perform tasks that are now virtually impossible, such as simulating complex molecules like protein folding and study molecule interactions for drug discovery, precision medicine, study of genomics, and research in the field of chemistry.

In the health and life sciences, quantum computers can help develop new treatments for diseases such as cancer, Alzheimer's, Parkinson's, and Alzheimer's. Researchers are already applying **Quantum Machine Learning** (QML) algorithms on healthcare records of individuals and trying to predict risk of developing heart and kidney diseases. Also, the current process of drug discovery using simulation techniques has a very high rate of failure and is time consuming in the clinical trials. The major scientific leap enabled by quantum computing in the field of drug discovery would be the accurate simulation of protein folding and their interactions with drugs and their behavior within our body cells.

Chapter 19

Quantum Computing in Cyber Security and Hacking

While companies and governments are continuously working to protect themselves against cybersecurity attacks with technological advances, the advent of the quantum computing system has created a revolution in this field. Cybersecurity experts are racing to introduce new forms of cryptography that would defend themselves against quantum hacks. As Google, IBM, and a couple of other companies became the first to develop fully functional quantum computers that have already been applied to practical problems, voices are growing louder warning that advances in technology could have very real unintended consequences.

Hackers who first get access to quantum computing technology can penetrate some of the most secure systems on the planet, potentially even crack blockchain encryption, and do anything to steal the most secure information on the planet and destabilize the cryptocurrency market.

It is hard to predict when the threat of quantum hacking might actually occur, but if scientists use quantum computers to solve useful problems, this could also pose serious problems for businesses and governments because it could potentially fall into the hands of threat scenarios. If it means that encrypted files could one day be decrypted, it could open the door to so-called *quantum hacking* attacks against companies, governments, or even the public at large. Quantum hacking will become a serious threat when quantum computers fall in the hand of criminals, as it will not only be able to defeat the current encryption systems but will also cause significant damage to other systems.

The power of quantum computing can potentially be used to easily hack into corporate networks and decrypt sensitive messages relatively easily. Today, hackers can intercept secure messages and use the mathematical power of quantum computation to crack encryption; this could create new vulnerabilities.

Eventually, it will be possible for the hackers to hack into networks, databases, and critical infrastructure systems without much resistance if they get access to Quantum Computing capabilities.

Now, the million-dollar question is can we really use quantum computing to build unbreakable mechanisms that are truly hack-proof. We already have a number of security protocols but ultimately, we will have to make cryptographic protocols with a problem that is hard to solve and withstand quantum attacks. It is important to understand that going forward protocols for information security essentially is not based on arithmetical compositions because those will no more be strong enough in front of a quantum computer.

To break such code, a conventional computer would need to achieve a much faster processing speed in the future than the best quantum computers available at that time. While hackers will have a hard time solving this problem on a **binary computer** (**BQP**) without quantum attacks, the processing speed that binary computers leave in the dust makes this solution obsolete.

In reality, a quantum computer is unlikely to be able to break RSA, and even less likely to cause serious damage to the system. Although quantum computing will take some more time to be widely available, governments and businesses must now begin to think about how to deal with emerging threats through appropriate post-quantum cryptography algorithms. The ability to withstand the computing power of a quantum computer is a critical part of any planning strategy that addresses the unique risks of cybersecurity.

Democratization of quantum computers is not as far away as the next level of technology, where cybersecurity could be seriously threatened. Until then, we will work on a post-quantum cryptography algorithm that claims to be able to protect data even beyond the capabilities of quantum computers.

CHAPTER 20

Quantum Computing in Movies and Cinemas

A long with all other industries, the movie industry worldwide is also going through a revolutionary transformation. This includes implementation of cutting-edge technologies at all stages of production, using digital means by replacing conventional production design, using modern technologies for bringing appealing visual reality and many more. It is clearly evident from the facts that more and more movies released today are 3D movies with advanced sound design and ready to run on different platforms, including OTT platforms.

Unlike in the past, now the success of a commercial movie depends on the budget for the technologies like Digital Set Design, VFX, Sound Design, Motion Capture, etc. Although engineers and mathematicians develop technologies and software that transform the film business and the experience of going to the cinema from time to time, now how Quantum Computing can give an extra mileage to modern movie making.

As we are glimpsing the power of quantum computing, the last couple of years have turned a trickle of interest from researchers into a stream. Recently, Google has achieved that quantum supremacy with their newly designed quantum computer. For Google in particular, quantum computing could help make its search engine more efficient, faster, and more accurate.

Quantum computing is based on Qubits that can represent both 1 and 0 simultaneously. It gives researchers the opportunity to bring scraps of data to their zero and 1 states, instead of cycling between them as with conventional digital computers. It is noteworthy that by adding an additional qubit, the process scales exponentially and quantum computers with two Qubits could perform up to four calculations at once or at least four times as many as a conventional computer.

This strange property means that quantum computers can perform calculations not individually, but simultaneously or parallelly. This enormous speed is crucial in many of the areas of Hi-Tech movie editing processes and special effects like VFX.

It is exciting to think that this real-time tool for film production will become more and more accepted and change the way films are made. Films in 3D are full of thoughts-changing stories, complex characters and complex plot twists.

While visuals often help explain complex concepts, Professor Peter Coveney is working with a large team at University College London on such work, and the potential applications of quantum computers could improve understanding of many of the world's most important scientific and technological problems including some related to visuals. We are at a point where we can justify the use of quantum computers for visual representations and special effects.

The real-time presentation consists of a live shoot with Technicolor's virtual production platform Genesis, which has already been successfully used in several film productions. To bridge the gap between the physical camera and its virtual counterpart, MPC has developed a rendering solution that is close to the functionality of conventional physical cameras.

This real-time technology allows the creators to have the project at hand at every stage of the process. This is a very interesting technology that really influences the way we perceive films. The assembling, editing, animating, and rendering has accelerated art and brought it a depth of reality that we would have thought possible. Have you ever thought about how far computers and visuals have come where visual effects were much dependent on making the images look good; we now have a whole new way of making movies with the use of virtual reality and immersive experience.

Filmmakers and their crew can work together on a live set, with a shared scene synchronized via a number of computers to synchronize shared scenes. Visual effects usually refer to the computer-generated objects that are done to enhance or alter the images so that the director can tell the story better. Photogrammetry is used where it is used to acquire assets with photorealistic accuracy. The footage is shot on the set and then in real time, using virtual reality.

To summarize, quantum computing will give a new dimension to both movie making as well as the experience watching a movie in an immersive and interactive manner.

CHAPTER 21
Quantum Computing in Spirituality and Mysticism

The quantum theory has become a strong scientific theory, but a group of people have begun to interpret it from an idealistic philosophical perspective as matter produced by the spirit. And Superstring Theory (M theory) continues to take quantum mysticism to a new level, while quantum theory is reinterpreted as a form of "spiritualism" and even as an alternative to the traditional "*scientific*" view of the universe. The ontological questions that arise about the nature of quantum systems and their relationship to nature make it difficult to distinguish between philosophical and scientific discussion.

Indian ancient great scriptures like Vedantas have described the nature of the universe and nature of human existence in a very profound manner which relates in many aspects to the quantum nature of the subatomic particles and the nature as a whole. Also, the concept of *all-pervading consciousness* which is called **Atman** or **Brahman** is essentially the quantum nature of the universe. Also, in many such ancient texts it has described the deep interconnectedness of all things in the universe not just the subatomic particles, which again is very similar to what we call quantum entanglement.

Since the 1970s, quantum mysticism has begun to go its own way by exploring the relationship between quantum physics and consciousness. *Fritjof Capra*, an eminent philosopher of the natural sciences, wrote his book *Tao of Physics* which explored the nature of quantum entanglement and its relationship to consciousness, and offered a new way of exploring it. In the 1980s, *Deepak Chopra's* book *Quantum Healing*, explaining the theory of mind-body healing using quantum concepts.

Tao of Physics (1975), which explored the nature of quantum entanglement and its relationship to consciousness as well as the relationship between quantum physics and consciousness in general. The quantum theory is undoubtedly one of the most important scientific theories in the history of science and philosophy that connects both the universe.

Quantum events are characterized by the concept of quantum computation and information theory, the so-called **quantum channels**. The corresponding quantum-inspired approach comprises a framework and uses formal features that are also used in quantum physics, such as quantum mechanics, quantum information, and quantum cryptography.

Quantum mysticism refers to a series of metaphysical ideas and related practices that are supposed to be related to the ideas of quantum mechanics and their interpretation. It is a collection of metaphysics, beliefs, and associated practice that strives to relate ideas from quantum mechanics and mechanics to their interpretations. The quantum field theory deals with a system with infinite degrees of freedom.

The philosophical and practices of quantum mysticism are based on philosophical interpretations and beliefs that correspond to the quantum theory and its corresponding philosophical interpretation and conviction. The idea that consciousness plays a role in quantum theory first emerged in the 1920s, when physicists such as *Albert Einstein, Max Planck* and *Friedrich Fysiks* turned to the idea of consciousness as an integral part of quantum field theory. Within a decade, the *Fundamental Fyik Group* was formed, a group of physicists who have devoted themselves to quantum mysticism in order to deal with the theoretical and practical implications of their theories and practices.

CHAPTER 22

Quantum Computing in Robotics

The secret of a quantum computer's power lies in its ability to generate and manipulate quantum qubits. The popular form of quantum computers is quantum logic gate systems that perform operations with qubits which is way faster than classic computing. This enormous computing speed is essentially going to be a boon for robotics and the other application that requires more computing power and parallel processing. Quantum computing driven by rapid prototyping processes lead to new possibilities in the field of robotics alongside machine learning and AI.

Harnessing the power of quantum computing technology will have a huge impact on deep learning AI and hence robotics. Artificial intelligence, which relies on processing large quantities of complex data sets is a fertile field for quantum computing. The quantum computing technology can reduce complexity and work with almost any search algorithm used in Robotics and AI applications. One of the most promising areas where quantum computing will have a major leap is for the training and processing of deep neural networks.

Quantum computers can be used to process quickly input data collected through cameras and sensors enabling Robots to identify the most important data points in the environment, such as temperature, humidity, wind speed, and other objects. From input capture to data collection and processing in a very fast speed quantum computers can be used to enable Robots to identify different types of objects, such as objects with different shapes, sizes, and shapes. The quantum computing technology can identify good places for sensors to incorporate sensors that capture the most significant data.

Also, the introduction of quantum computers to the online market in the form of cloud services can one day enable the development of new types of robotic systems by the developer communities worldwide.

Given the growing importance of quantum computing technology in the field of learning combined with its potential for human-machine interaction, it is obvious that at least some of our advanced robots of the future will be controlled by a quantum computer and quantum computing technology will be leveraged as a means of building robots.

CHAPTER 23

Quantum Computing in Nuclear Research and Study of Atoms

For decades, theoretical physicists and computer scientists have been collecting evidence that quantum computers will eventually leave the current supercomputers in the dust. Quantum computers have the potential to transform modern life by using their ability to solve complex problems such as atomic research and nuclear physics. The power of a quantum computer is generated by leveraging the properties of subatomic particles, the feature like superposition and entanglement.

Using a web connection to a remote quantum device, the researchers performed a quantum calculation of the binding energy of deuterons. In the laboratory, the team performed quantum calculations on the nuclear binding state of neutrons, a key component of nuclear physics.

A study led by physicists describes how a technique called quantum annealing can be used to solve complex problems in nuclear research such as the construction of nuclear reactors. This ground-breaking discovery has a far-reaching impact on many applications of quantum computing. Quantum computers promise to solve many of the problems of calculating the structure of molecules, atoms, and atomic nuclei, etc. Also, Quantum Field Theory could be simulated to study the most fundamental nature of the universe, including simulating nuclear test environment.

A California based company, Rigetti Computing, is providing the full stack of quantum computing capabilities required to build the **superconducting quantum materials and systems center (SQMS)** quantum computer. IBM Quantum is working with the center to develop the critical building blocks for this mission, such as quantum interconnection technology that connects individual processors and potentially allows quantum computers to scale to a great extent. Rigetti Computing's cloud-based quantum computing platform and simulator is working for the SQMS quantum computer and a number of other quantum systems and applications. While this funding focuses on nuclear physics, the resulting algorithms can benefit other areas that want to capitalize on the promise of the quantum computing technology to solve complicated problems more quickly.

Northwest Quantum Nexus (NQN) supported by the Office of Nuclear Physics of DOE, the project aims to develop quantum tools for nuclear research and to contribute expertise in nuclear physics to quantum systems. It's developing advanced large-format quantum computers that use state-of-the-art scientific algorithms developed by researchers. This research area is called computer architecture and involves the conception of how a quantum computer would interact with existing technologies and what types of software would be compatible with quantum systems.

Chapter 24

Quantum Computing in Sports and Games

Sports is obviously a physical activity, and it was always believed that there is very little a computer can do to change that, except to make it easier. However, the performance enhancement by computer systems of an athlete does not violate the rules of the sports association and is permitted in the world of competitive sports.

A gaming company, NEX has developed a solution that uses computer vision and machine learning to analyze the skills of basketball players. It's now planning to use Quantum Computing to further strengthen the solution. Each player's solution in Quantum Motion is sent to a team of researchers who then use the data to optimize the actual manipulation of qubits for further research and optimization.

Also, one might wonder what a quantum computer will do for video games, given that the current state of quantum games is basically just glorified random number generators. Just start a game with a state-of-the-art quantum computer and it works just as good as any other games. However, as quantum computing becomes more sophisticated, quantum games will be one of the first areas in which quantum computers finally gain a quantum advantage.

The companies such as Google, IBM, Microsoft, that are working aggressively on more and more powerful quantum computers, hope that one day they will truly revolutionize the way we interact with computers and with the video games.

Although quantum games today are primarily about solving puzzles etc., but in the coming few years, you will see many games like Fortnite in the gaming world, which were actually developed for quantum computers. Players will be able to use an open source framework like IBM's quantum computing, which will provide everyone with access to quantum computers in the cloud. In fact, it will be first of its kind for games that integrate quantum computing into their gameplay.

A program that puts IBM's quantum computers in the cloud and gives developers and scientists the opportunity to play with the quantum world. At the same time, IBM introduces its users to the quantum experience which allows people without a physics degree to write their own games. As for the success of quantum video games, a game developed for a 5-qubit quantum computer and the IBM Qiskit Open-Source Framework with the Python computer language is another kind of success. Other areas are quantum computing educational games that allow break down of quantum principles so that audiences without a scientific background can explore concepts in a fun environment.

In *Hello Quantum* for example, the player unknowingly plays a quantum computer game with a 5-qubit or a 3-qubit computer. This suggests that games with quantum computers can be an important step in raising public awareness of the technology. James Wootton, an IBM researcher, developed this technique as part of his research into how quantum computers can generate the content of games.

Already a game with a state-of-the-art quantum computer has just been released in the US and Europe for PlayStation 4 and Xbox One. Wootton developed a game to compare the quantum computer with other classical computers called **Quantum Awesomeness**.

CHAPTER 25

Quantum Computing in Traffic Optimization

As the population of vehicles in the cities has been increasing, the traffic management has becoming increasingly complex and, in many cities, it has become practically impossible to manage it properly. By 2030, almost 50% of world's population will start living in cities and this will require a huge transformation of the infrastructure of our cities. The future smart cities will be highly dependent of the massive amount of data generated from the smart IOT devices embedded across to make the cities smarter. To process and analyze this humongous amount of data for real-time insights and decision-making using AI, it will be very difficult with a classical computing approach alone. Quantum computing can exponentially change the smart cities landscape by processing this vast amount of data efficiently real-time in association with classical computers. It is going to revolutionize the management of road infrastructure, critical assets, and capacity planning that will result in higher levels of service, better community management, and improve infrastructure management and optimization of resources of the smart cities. The quantum computing approach is the best approach for route optimization and offers a healthy traffic management leading to a smarter traffic ecosystem.

Volkswagen has successfully demonstrated the use of quantum computers for traffic optimization in the area of traffic management by optimizing traffic routes. Also, in another project, D-Wave's quantum computer was used to calculate the fastest route for each bus in real time in a city. It calculates faster routes for individual buses by taking into account factors such as the number of buses, the distance between buses, and the speed of traffic and other factors. The computational principles of quantum computers are particularly well suited to this kind of projects because they solve optimization problems natively. In addition to simulations, quantum computing could solve complex problems such as those that require extremely fast processing and find the best optimum solution out of an enormous number of potential solutions. This is expected to lead to solving a number of real problems in the automotive industry. The best example is the classic *Optimizing itineraries for traveling salesmen.*

The transportation sector is looking at quantum computing to make traffic management and public transportation systems more efficient and congestion free. Devices like drones, sensors, cameras, robots, self-driving vehicles, traffic signals, and others collect data every day on traffic flow and inhabited area. Instead of using all that data to assess one option at a time, quantum computers can simultaneously assess a multitude of options. It reduces the overall time to solution. Traffic route optimization will reduce road collisions and congestion by applying the same principle. Volkswagen is working on the same use case of mobility of the future by utilizing QC-based optimizations to make traffic management smarter for cities. Similarly, Ford Motors is leveraging Microsoft Quantum computing capabilities for congestion mitigation solution to be inbuilt in Ford vehicles that will help to avoid congestions to individual vehicle and overall traffic.

CHAPTER 26
Quantum Computing in Metaverse

There are several definitions of Metaverse and imaginations in people's mind that what shape and form it will take in the future, and its practical utility beyond the dystopian outlook. I personally see Metaverse is evolving as the biggest virtual marketplace, the largest business epicenter, and the coolest entertainment hub in another five to ten years timeframe. And I am not exaggerating because if we look back in the past, especially in the technological world; the innovation and adoption goes skyrocketing if the concept has all the ingredients to touch the common mass. And trust me, Metaverse has all those ingredients. Alongside, the other ingredients like decentralized currencies built on blockchain, community ownership, **non-fungible tokens (NFTs)**, Web3.0 and virtual/augmented/mixed reality making it more diversified and practical for a virtual business world to take a palpable shape.

More than just a virtual world, metaverse is going to obliterate the physical limitations that we as humans have. A simplistic example is many times we want to be physically present at many places at the same time but due to our physical limitation that's never going to be feasible. Now, with our digital twins in the metaverse, it's very much possible to be at multiple places at the same time in the virtual world. The same goes for the business world; you can expect a completely democratic, decentralized global business platform for you irrespective of the size and nature of your business. Already many experts have forecasted that businesses in the digital platform like in metaverse will outperform the conventional businesses. Although almost all the businesses that exist in the planet and that we can think of can be and will be exported to metaverse in future; however, I would like to segregate those to immediate, mid-term, and long-term transition in the metaverse.

The immediate opportunities that have already started happening in the metaverse are grand events, concerts, and fashion shows taking place in metaverse and millions of audiences are viewing and participating in those through immersive experiences. The entertainment and fashion industry futurists have already understood the importance of such platforms and are investing hugely for placement of their products and advertising their brands in the metaverse. Fashion brands like Nike, Balenciaga, Charli Cohen and entertainment houses like Disney are already ahead in the race. The other area that is already in trend is buying and selling of digital assets and products and this is an emerging market in the metaverse. This brings to the table a unique concept which is going to revolutionize the digital business called *Digital-Only* products or assets.

Collaboration like creating co-working places for meetings, conferencing, brainstorming, trainings, and tradeshows in a simulated interactive environment has also started happening in metaverse, like Facebook's horizon and few others have recently tried those concepts.

And needless to mention that for online gamers and game developers metaverse is a heaven. The online gaming world is already a booming industry; it's bigger than the music and movie industries combined and metaverse will make it even bigger. Along with games another industry which is already going through a revolutionary transformation is the Social Media business. The reason being, as Facebook is transforming itself into Meta, a completely virtual 3D-based immersive kind of platform in the metaverse; the other social media platforms are bound to move into metaverse or provide users similar experience to sustain in the competition. The same applies for the e-commerce and social commerce; either they will have to move their shops to some existing metaverse, or they will have to build their own metaverse and operate from there.

Travel and tourism and leisure and hospitality industries will have no other options but to partner with metaverse companies and place their stores in metaverse because tourists of future would like to have that pre-booking virtual immersive experience of the sites before even booking their tours. Metaverse is also going to be the biggest and cheapest platform for advertisement irrespective of the nature of your business.

In the healthcare industry, many areas are getting revolutionized, including practical classes and trainings using VR technologies, including medical procedures and surgeries. Metaverse is going to lay the foundation of the global virtual healthcare industry and its adoption across geographics. Doctors and healthcare professionals can collaborate and share experiences real-time during any procedure. Using oculus, VR headset effective management of COVID patients was tried out by Meta in collaboration with WHO Academy during the pandemic.

The banking and finance industry will also rush to metaverse soon once the virtual marketplace in metaverse attracts popularity. Financial industry will try to catch up with the parallel financial world of emerging digital economy and the metaverse is the right place for the banks and financial institutions to display their digital products and services.

Last but not the least, the business around building the metaverse itself and developing ultramodern light-weight wearables like headsets, glasses and contact lenses is also going to flourish in the coming years. Similarly, there will be a huge job opportunity for the 3D designers, game developers, data scientists, metaverse architects, blockchain developers, industry specific domain experts, publishers, advertisers, creative people, and many more. Metaverse has already been able to attract the attention of the investors. Many investors both angel and venture capitals find it the coolest place to invest their funds to safeguard their investment from the volatility of the physical world.

When it comes to India, India's largest IT services company, **Tata Consultancy Services (TCS)** has already made investments in Metaverse. Facebook's CEO Mark Zuckerberg has said that India will play a huge part in building the metaverse with the country's huge developer base, which will become the largest in the world by 2024. Indian metaverse Zionverse has launched its NFT named Lakshmi recently. Indian startups and developer communities will play a major role in this revolution and there will be huge business opportunities in the Indian IT ecosystem at large. The Indian Government recently declared the plan for 5G and other emerging technologies and clarified its stand on digital assets and digital currencies which will provide further boost in terms of adoption and investment in metaverse and other peripherical areas.

CHAPTER 27

Quantum Computing in Fintech, AI, and Sustainability

B anks vs Fintechs is a hot topic today and there are a whole lot of speculations and schools of thoughts going around this topic. On one hand, the fintech firms are aggressively intruding into the territories of the banks, taking over traditional banking functions; on the other hand, we are also seeing some of the success stories of fintech firms joining hands with the banks complementing each other, and thereby offering brilliant services to the customers.

As per some experts, it's going to be a tough competition initially but someday in the future eventually, there could be convergence among the traditional banks and these next-gen financial institutions, the *Fintechs*. I personally believe that fundamentally there was a gap that existed, and it exists even today between what customers expect and what banks can deliver. Fintechs seized the opportunity in addressing these gaps. One example is partnering with banks or independently; they provide a frictionless digital banking experience that customers would have been expecting from the banks since long.

Nevertheless, the fintech phenomena have far reaching impacts. It is not only transforming the traditional financial services but fintechs are already playing a major role in revolutionizing sustainable finance or sustainability at large. Fintech has a great power; it brings together the power of technology along with finance and uses it for building sustainable future of the planet.

On a broader spectrum, fintechs are transforming sustainable development in finance in three different ways. Firstly, using the power of Internet, mobile technologies, big data, and artificial intelligence, it has been able to enhance the digital reach of financial services to those segments of population that did not have access to the services through traditional channels. For example, Financial Inclusion is one of those areas where fintechs have played a major role by bringing a large section of unbanked population under the financial umbrella using disruptive digital technologies. Also, rendering financial services and making those available to the customers wherever they are available like mobile banking, social banking, WhatsApp banking, etc. are probably some of the biggest attempts towards sustainability and green finance.

Out of all other technologies in this spectrum, AI has a special role to offer, and it has already been leveraged by most of the Fintech firms in many of their products and solutions. The ability of AI is in perfect sync with the need of sustainable finance in many ways. It includes powering solutions to provide affordable services anywhere anytime; eliminating physical aspects by delivering through digital means, and the personalization and predictive capabilities of AI makes it the first choice for the FinTech firms and the Financial Institutions today.

The second major impact that fintechs have been able to make is by bringing down the cost of financial services and making it affordable for even the lowest income category of the society by using newgen technologies. It has also been able to break the monopolies of some of the financial institutions and bring competition in terms of cost.

And the third contribution is the innovative approach of serving customers through digital channels and touchpoints keeping customer convenience at the center. They eliminated the complexities around security, privacy, regulatory, and compliance matters from the customer journey while providing a bouquet of financial services to the customers.

Looking at it through a sustainability lens is very important when it comes to any financial initiative to make it a successful green finance project. This dimension must be taken into consideration seriously. While selecting products, services, or partners or even while making investments, sustainability is a factor that has now been investigated very seriously as one of the critical parameters. Experts are now convinced that fintech can play an important role encouraging impact investment or sustainable investment.

Associating sustainable goals with fintech initiatives may not be easy by getting started will start having an impact gradually. Even while doing technological innovations in any field, we should always keep in mind the aspects of sustainability. By encouraging fintech initiatives, sustainable finance is getting encouraged indirectly.

For example, a quantitative analysis and representation of what contributions an individual has done by choosing a sustainable alternative is very important to encourage people for exploring sustainable options in every walk of life. Fintech can solve this easily by integrating sustainable options and displaying qualifiable impact that's of a buying decision or any other decisions for that matter.

It's high time for every business today to come forward and not only support sustainability by principle but also integrate sustainability in their business models and the goals. Technology can actually help materializing those sustainability goals and Fintech in Finance is already showcasing a perfect example to the world.

CHAPTER 28

How Quantum Explains Human Consciousness?

Although I have been hearing these spiritual jargons like "The Consciousness", "The Self" (*Atman* - in Sanskrit language), from my grandparents since my childhood, but due to my ignorance or whatever, I never paid any attention nor did I took any serious attempt to even understand the deeper meaning of those terminologies. Honestly, I kept aside those spiritual items for my retirement life.

Incidentally, few years back while digging into some deeper concepts of quantum physics, somehow, I confronted with the so-called *The Self* (The Consciousness or Atman) again somewhere in a book. But this time, I could not ignore it. The more I went deeper into understanding the concepts from different books, I found it so profound and rational that it compelled and dragged me hostile into a revolutionary thought process that I had never experienced in the past. To my astonishment, these concepts started challenging my each and every concept of the *Material World* and the *Classical Physics* exactly the way when I did started understanding the concepts of quantum physics many years back.

I will try to share my understanding about the self or pure consciousness in this chapter. I would also like to highlight here that this is not a spiritual or religious chapter, nor does any attempt has been made to uphold any particular religion or mysticism. Let's take few steps back to understand the concepts better.

The mystery of our existence and the fundamental nature of the universe compelled the human being time to time to explore the unknown and the truth in many different ways since time immemorial.

Out of those many approaches, the evident-based and experiment oriented approach flourished as "Science" as we know it today keeping its entire focus on exploring the material world; which latter branched into technology that centered around the application of science to solve real-world problems in many different areas aimed for the betterment of humanity.

On the other hand, another approach continued to explore the other dimensions that are *Not Perceivable by our Six Senses*, or the dimensions beyond the material world. Surprisingly, the practitioners of this approach somehow convinced that there exists other dimensions that are beyond the scope of what we perceive through our sense organs. They also realized the fact that it needs a different method altogether to explore such detentions and cannot be accessed through material means or tools. I would say, this realization by itself was a great invention at that time which took a couple of thousand years to be realized and accepted by a group of classical physicists today.

Astonishingly, the outcome of such explorations of the unknown dimensions resulted in some amazing findings that can be directly correlated with the modern Quantum Physics and quantum behavior of subatomic particles. I will try to highlight only a few of those in this article.

It was highlighted that the core of the material world is actually non-matter, and it manifests into material form, to be precise, it's just a manifestation or we can even say an illusion. Quantum physics today says exactly the same thing which we have been completely missing before in classical physics.

To put it straight, we were so engrossed with the material world and its exploration that we missed out a very fundamental deeper dimension which is non-material in nature. This non-material dimension that manifests itself into material frame of our body is explained as our *Consciousness* or *Atman*, the true essence of who we are beyond our physical or social identity. It also holds good for non-leaving being, and that is what exactly Quantum physics indicates - every matter has a non-matter nature at its core; and the phenomena it apparently exhibits is just the epiphenomena (a secondary or just a byproduct).

Now, we can correlate this with what is written and available in some of the ancient texts that this non-matter dimension that exists within human or any living being is *Not Perishable or Destroyable*; because those applies to only material things like our biological body. The non-matter aspect within us remains unaffected even after our Biological Death. So, what that means is there exists something even after our death. Isn't it amazing? In fact, this is the core of all religions that exists in this planet. The core of any religion, spirituality, or mysticism is based on the belief that *There is something that is beyond our death.*

Our pure consciousness which is non-matter in nature remains and manifests again into some material frame, probably acquires a new life. This theory or hypothesis explains the consciousness much convincingly then what biological or medical science explains. As per medical science, our consciousness is consequence of the complex neural activities in our brain, but that doesn't explain many other fundamental things like quantum challenging traditional scientific view of the universe and the material world today.

We will explore a few deeper dimensions like how pure consciousness or the self is *All-Pervading* (meaning everywhere) and what is the quantum explanation of the same in the next book.

Index